CHURCH FATHERS

VS

KINGDOM SONS

Inheritance Worth Fighting For

Charles L. Coker Jr.

Burkhart Books
Bedford, Texas

Copyright © 2013 Charles Coker Jr.
Published in the United States of America
ISBN: 978-0-9859908-8-6
Library of Congress Control Number: 2013933741
Published in the United States of America, 2013
Burkhart Books 2013, Bedford, TX

All rights reserved as permitted under the U. S. Copyright Act of 1976. No part of this publication may be reproduced, distributed, or transmitted in any form or by any means, or stored in a database or retrieval system, without the expressed written permission of the author and publisher.

Unless otherwise indicated, all Scripture is taken from The New King James Version. Copyright © 1982 by Thomas Nelson, Inc. Used by permission. All rights reserved.

Holy Bible, New International Version®, NIV® Copyright © 1973, 1978, 1984, 2011 by Biblica, Inc.® Used by permission. All rights reserved worldwide.

Edited by: MaryAnn Royal, Cari Cusick, and Philomene Royal.
Cover Design: Hudsen Smith, www.injectantidote.com

Burkhart Books
Bedford, Texas
www.burkhartbooks.com

What Others Are Saying about This Book:

Too often, when the rumbling starts in our lives, we run, hide, avoid, and deny that our failure to accept responsibility for our actions is the root cause of most of our problems. My son Charles has outlined what has worked for us in the last few years. His decision to deal with it in print is a blessing to me and, hopefully, will be to you.

Charles L. Coker Sr.
Author's Father

I cannot begin to say how proud I am of my husband, for persevering through the obstacles that could have stopped him from writing this book. We have had many unique adventures through our 33 years of marriage. Not all of them were joyous occasions, but they have been beneficial for our journey. I can truly say that once Charlie grasped the Father's love through sonship, I watched him transform into his true calling. As you read this book and apply the principles, it will help bring clarity to who you truly are and were designed to be.

Susan G. Coker
Wife of a Great Man!

Charlie is one of only a few men I would trust with my life. I met him in 2007 and have walked with him in the kingdom since then. I remember a man coming to me with such promise but also with an orphan spirit. Many men struggle with this but don't really know it. Dealing with the issues of our broken expectations is vital for a healthy existence. In this book you will hear of the extraordinary love of God, and you will see how one man found his way from orphan to son. Knowing Charlie has been one of the great joys of my life. Many times I have tapped into the wisdom of God that resides with him. The different levels of anointing and grace that Charlie has moved into have been nothing less than extraordinary. In all of that, the thing I treasure the most is our friendship. Few people have the character to walk in covenant to the degree that Charlie will walk in it with you. That kind of friendship everyone should experience. I recommend this book, and I highly recommend this man. His ministry of love and power will greatly impact your life for heaven's glory.

Louis C. DeSiena
Senior Leader-The Gate Fellowship-Jacksonville, FL

I found this book to be very interesting reading, and it is written to be understood by the average reader. Charlie Coker is truly an impressionist writer. As he recalls an account, he articulates with words that never leave you scratching your head in wonder of what he is saying or trying to convey. The stories and experiences revealed in this book are used to assist the reader in opening a powerful revelation to all church fathers who have been cheated of their destinies, and have struggled to fulfill all the wondrous things God has had for them. As the church moves forward with God's seal of approval upon its labors, it needs this fresh word.

Dr. Rev. Phillip J. Casterline
Living Waters Church Hornell, New York

I have known, respected, and watched the maturity of Charlie for 13 yrs. I am honored to be mentioned in this book; I am referred to as "the horse's butt, by the proverbial tree of contention" in Round Seven. Your friends tell you what you want to hear; a mentor tells you what you need to hear. Fathers mentor with patience, walking along beside you, showing you how to get it right. We definitely have much in common now. I truly love this guy. His brutal honesty has been tempered by the continual spankings from the Holy Spirit's School of wisdom. It has produced a patient father, loving leader, and great friend. As you read this book, I challenge you to get ready to hear his amazing journey from humility to authority.

Reggie Parker
Mighty Warriors Ministries

After you read this amazing story of Charlie's life in ministry, you will clearly see that God intends to use you right where you are. You can be a weapon to bring restoration to dysfunctional people, orphans, and those with a religious spirit. This book will help you to understand that what you are walking through, as tough as it is, is what God is using to mold and shape you into what God needs you to be. Whatever paradigm you are currently in, (the local church, a house church, the apostolic, prophetic, evangelical, or denominational), God wants you as a son. This book will speak to your situation and help you understand how intimately God is involved in all your circumstances and situations. He uses us perfectly where we are, to get us to where we need to be, if we are willing. Thank you, Charlie, for so transparently giving us the insight into your life, your journey, and our Father who so amazingly takes us from glory to glory.

Pastor Brian Higbee
Sr. Pastor CityChurch, Connellsville, PA

I read the original draft, and Charlie is very straightforward. He tells it like it is. The raw truth; I like it that way. It has been a long, and sometimes hard, journey for him to get to the truth, but I believe he has been successful. You may not always agree with how he deals with people, but you can always see his heart. I believe you will benefit greatly from this book.

Pastor Buddy Tipton
Central Assembly of God, Vero Beach, FL

Acknowledgments

This book is dedicated to my wife Susie, who has walked with me, prayed for me, and loved me, in spite of who I was. Your incredible strength and wisdom have shown me a window into God's love that is irreplaceable. I will never forget the day God told me that you didn't decide to stay married to me because of me. It was because you trusted Him and your obedience to God. After all I had done to salvage this marriage and family, that was a true kick in the pants! Thanks for loving and trusting God more than you did me. We are truly blessed to have our sons, Jason and Bryan, in our lives. Thanks, Guys, for being patient, while Mom and Dad tried to divorce, and God wouldn't let us. You guys are the best. Remember the family motto: *"If you're going to be dumb, you had better be tuff!"* Love you!

Also, I need to thank my mother, Onalee, and my father, Charles, and three older sisters, Becky, Margaret and Pam. I know it was hard being raised in a family with the youngest being Mom's favorite. But, I pray a blessing over you to get healed from rejection.

To MaryAnn Royal, thanks for putting up with me all the years you have tried to make me look excellent on paper in both redneck and English. You could not have done this book with me, if you had not seen my heart, and for that I am grateful.

To Cari Cusick, what a job it has been teaching a scholar like you to discern redneck. Thank you for the labor of love you have given us for the completion of the book.

Contents

What Others Are Saying about This Book:	3
Acknowledgments	6
Foreword by Charles Coker Sr.	9
Foreword by Jack Taylor	11
Preface	13
Introduction	15

Personal Authority

Why My Father!	21
The Place of My Birth	35
Living for Jesus, Baptist Style	43
Leave Your Father's House	51

Church Authority

Surviving the Snakes of Church and Not Becoming One Yourself	65
The Word of Faith Church	69
Being Sent to a Man, not a Church	79

Apostolic Authority

What Do You Do When Your Reality Check bounces?	97
Who's in Charge, Father or Son?	115

Kingdom Authority

The Younger Brother!	133
A Trip to China with My Dad	145
Birthing the Church	157

Sonship Authority

You Don't Know Jack, Until You Know Jack	169
Multiplication by Death	185
Bringing Heaven to Earth	195
The Power of Redeemed Orphans!	207

Foreword by Charles Coker Sr.

On a hot summer day, my son, the author of this book, asked me to let him take our lawn mower and mow a neighbor's lawn. He was ten years old at the time. I allowed him to do it. He came home totally wet with sweat. He was holding three dollars in his hand and said, "Daddy, I wish I had all the lawns in the world to mow." This episode pretty much describes his personality and motivational make up. "Full speed ahead and damn the torpedoes!!!" In many cases it has served him well; however, his book gives an overview of the folly of running from God and leaving Him out of our lives.

In his middle teen years we would go face to face about some of his and his friends' shenanigans. Even though our discussions would become heated, we were able to communicate without berating one another or getting physical. I would tell him I loved him, "You are mine; you are my son. No matter what you do, I still love you!" He could have given me a hard time physically, but he did not. God is good!

In early 1978, I was sent by the postal service to work in New Orleans, Louisiana. This assignment lasted for several weeks. In February, I received a letter from my son. I cherish this letter and have it in front of me as I write. My grandson was born March 14, 1978. Charles, my son, turned 19 on June 22. Charles and Susie were married in 1980.

With my son's permission, I share some of his statements and expressions from his letter.

"Dear Father:
I am in a private place doing a lot of thinking. I know I am "bull-headed" (his words) and don't always do what you would like me to do. When I was growing up I felt you were too strict and unfair at times. Looking back I see that I was a problem, or would have been if I had not had a firm hand on my back. I could have turned out a lot worse. You stood up for what you believed and never gave up. Dad, what I am trying to say is, I love you very much and know you are behind me all the way.
                                                    Love,
                                                        your son."

In the 1980's my son was making a lot of money in the lighting business, and as a family we had good fellowship and good times together. But when he was invited to church, we were mostly ignored. My wife confronted Charles about his ungodly lifestyle, and she got away with it. When I prayed about it, God spoke to me and said, "Stop bugging him. He has his idols. Leave him alone!" This I did for nearly five years, but God led me to pray for my son like Job did. In Job 1:5, Job prayed for his sons and interceded before God on their behalf.

The last 14 years of service in the post office, I was in management. My job, for the most part, was to see to it that other people did their job in a correct and timely manner. As a deacon in the church, I witnessed many parents cutting their children too much slack and leaving an open door to misbehave, and that was harmful to the child in the long run. I do not doubt that these life assignments had some effect on how I acted and reacted as a parent and father.

For the past 14 years, I have ministered in the jail and 4 prisons. Two of these are maximum-security prisons. There are men in these facilities who will never walk the streets again. Yet, because they have invited Jesus into their lives, they have a life worth living even in prison. This has been the most satisfying time of my Christian life. I do not throw the church under the bus. It definitely has its place in God's plan.

Here we are in 2013. My son has matured into a man with a passion to bring healing into the lives of those who are hurting.

We are on the same page concerning things that really matter. Believe it or not, I have mellowed out a little.

To God be the Glory

Charles Layton Coker Sr.
Charlie's Dad

Foreword by Jack Taylor

Charlie Coker became a spiritual son of mine through a series of events that have the rare fragrance of the miraculous. He is one among many sons whom I treasure and trust. Every time I am with him I am impressed at the magnitude of the ministry God has given him. Whether I am buying a book or writing an introduction, preface or foreword, I first lean toward the author. If I find a man of integrity toward his fellow man, a passion toward God, and a pattern of straightforward truth telling, I build on that sure foundation. I find all these qualities in Charlie Coker.

Now to his book with the fetching title, *Church Fathers vs. Kingdom Sons*. Even if I were a total stranger to this manuscript and only faintly acquainted with Charlie, my curiosity would, nevertheless, have been captured. My deepening acquaintance with the author serves only to multiply my intrigue. The statements that flank the title are valid additions to the subject matter. Above the title the searching question challenges the reader with the words, "Are You Ready to Rumble?" Below the title identifies the expected result of reading this strategic material, "Inheritance Worth Fighting For" as in Round 1, Round Two, etc...

You, my dear reader, are about to receive a shocking challenge in your life as you engage in Kingdom principles with the Kingdom's operating system: the Father-Son paradigm. In my humble and decisive opinion, herein lies the problem of the modern church: the absence of Kingdom mentality This volume is not so much a study of the Kingdom of God, as it is a map of one life under the Holy Spirit's direction that led the seeker to a head-on collision with the eternal Kingdom of God. The result: a happy fanatic!

It is obvious that Charlie Coker is somewhere between slightly and seriously decisive and hard-headed about everything. No lesson he has learned, has been learned without God's decisive action in his life, that speaks of a 12 pound sledge hammer applied to the forehead just above the eyes and directly between the ears. This amazing story is chronicled in surprisingly easy-to-understand language that sometimes comes through with a mild hint of profanity. The author is not content with just writing something to fill the page, but is only satisfied with saying what he writes in the toughest trappings of bald clarity. The reader is apt to experience a reaction with the thought, "Did I just read what I think I read?" My answer to that query is, "You should have read the original manuscript!" The manuscript required many visits to the etymological washateria, (a word-usage laundromat), in order to prevent serious offense to the average reader. In editing the book we have sought to take the keen edge off words that were bound to shock and offend, and substitute more delicate words that still convey the thoughts needed for the occasion. We think we have done a good job in this needed endeavor.

Charlie Coker is not a seasoned scholar or theologian but a maturing disciple seriously in love with Jesus. He is the kind of novel thinker who will shake the intelligentsia of the church world and roughly disturb religion in general! By the way, he is not a poor scholar or a bad theologian!

I predict a wide reading of this volume and, in the wake of its reading, a long line of changed lives, awakened passions and redirected purposes. I will close my contribution here with, "Attaboy, Charlie. You done good!"

Thanks, Susie, for staying with Charlie when anybody else would have flown the coop. You have trained him well!

Dr. Jack Taylor
Dimensions Ministries
Melbourne, FL
April, 2013

Preface

You've picked up this book wondering, why is this author picturing the church, the body of Christ, in a boxing match? It doesn't make sense. The church is supposed to be in unity and love everyone.

This is the story of my personal journey from being a spiritual orphan to becoming the begotten, spiritual son of the Most High God. This journey started 20 years ago with my first supernatural encounter with Jesus. As God took me step by step, He taught me what not to do, so I could see clearly what to do. As you progress through this book, I urge you to "do as I say, and not as I do (did)." Following the Kingdom Keys can lead you into Sonship and a fresh relationship with the Lord.

As I've traveled along this often unpaved road, I have observed *church fathers* (leaders in the churches I attended) and the consequences of them being spiritual orphans. Many church fathers have missed their destinies, never fulfilling all the wonders God has had for them to receive and accomplish, because they never understood His love. They continued in the patterns they learned from those before them. They were sons of their fathers. I've seen that there is no greater sin committed by church leaders, than repeating the sin that was committed against them. God holds those in leadership accountable for repeating the sins of their fathers. So the boxing match begins.

You have your own personal journey that you are destined to walk. It is ultimately your choice whether you walk as a *church father* or a **Kingdom Son.** If you choose the way of Sonship, there is much from my journey that you can glean and apply to your own life, making your journey easier and quicker. Let's rumble!

Introduction

Church Fathers vs. Kingdom Sons

Wow, what a beautiful day! I'm on my way to Houston, Texas to spend the weekend with Papa Jack Taylor. My mind is churning, wondering how Jack and his son, Tim, will receive me.

Is this spiritual Sonship thing for real? I know what the scriptures say in Malachi 4:5-6:

Behold, I will send you Elijah the prophet before the coming of the great and dreadful day of the Lord. And he will turn the hearts of the fathers to the children, And the hearts of the children to their fathers, Lest I come and strike the earth with a curse.

But is it really going to work this time? I was thinking about my father, and all the pastors and authorities that God had given me to submit to over the years. They had, for the most part, all ended in some kind of disappointment. It started with my own dad, who kept me at arm's length for years before he accepted that I "might" be a man of God. It continued with the *church fathers* (leaders of churches I was a part of), who could care less about you, if you were not under their authority, building their mountain of influence. It didn't matter if it was God who was moving you to go somewhere else; you became obsolete and discarded.

Then I got the phone call that changed everything. It was Dad, my earthly, biological father. He asked me what I was doing, and why I was going to Houston. I told him I was on the way to the airport to spend the weekend with Papa Jack, my spiritual father.

My father said that he was really thankful that Jack was in my life, "I believe that he is an answer to the prayers I've prayed for you for years. I desired that you would have somebody of his caliber who would really help you in ministry. I am very thankful, as God has answered my prayers."

As Dad took credit for Jack Taylor coming into my life, this ungodly anger started to erupt inside of me. The anger of an orphan; that deep anger that hurts in the gut. That pain deep down inside of me started coming to the surface. It was rage! It was resentment; rebellion; and hatred, yes, even hatred. **Remember, hate is what love is not.** This level of dishonor had not been allowed to surface like that in a long time, but there it was, coming to the forefront of my heart. It looked very ugly and sinful. All of these emotions rushed to the surface at one time. I've had them before, but I've always suppressed them because I'm a 51-year-old father with two natural sons, and several spiritual sons. I'm also a pastor and a traveling minister. "Honor thy father and mother that your days will be long, and all will go well with thee;" you know, that commandment stuff. I thanked Dad for the prayers and said I would call him next week.

Why did it make me so angry? Sorry God, I must still have some issue with him taking credit for Jack coming into my life. After all, if he had been the man of God he should have been, I would not have needed Jack Taylor.

As we arrived in Houston, I met up with my friend, who is a spiritual son of Leif Hetland. Leif was putting on the conference. After we got settled into our hotel, I called Jack about supper and the meeting arrangements for the night. Leif Hetland, Jack, and others of high respect in the Christian community, were the speakers that weekend. Here was my prayer for the weekend, "Dear Lord, give me favor with Jack and others. Please help me not to be an embarrassment to Jack or to You. Help me speak with wisdom and grace, and not look like the dumb redneck I feel like most of the time."

The first night Jack spoke, he introduced me to the crowd and told them I was one of his newest spiritual sons. He gave a favorable review on how we met and that I was one of his "stranger" sons because of the gifting I carry. With that public affirmation after he spoke, he called Tim, Leif, Kris Vallotton, and me to the front to pray for people. As I looked at the crowds, there were as many people wanting prayer from me as the others. I looked at the people lined up in front of me for prayer, and I heard the Lord speak, "This is your inheritance; welcome to Sonship. Now pray with the authority of heaven."

As we were finishing the evening, we made plans for the next day.

We looked at Jack's speaking schedule. He told me that there was a workshop at the same time he was speaking, and that he wanted me to go learn how to SOAK. I said, "I don't soak." Jack answered, "I know. That's the problem!" I tried to debate, but that didn't work to my advantage at all. Whining and trying to work my way out of it didn't help. I hate to lean back or lay down, and soaking is for sissies! Jack told me that I needed to learn to lean back. There he goes again! That's all he ever says, "Lean back;" that's all he has said to me in over a year of this spiritual fathering stuff. I have waited for some correction, great wisdom, or even discipline; a little spanking to straighten me out. All he has ever said is, "Learn to lean back." "I don't lean back!" I said. Jack shot back, "That's my point, son, that's my point."

I fretted all night. I really wanted to hear Jack speak and didn't like the soaking part. After I did my morning prayers, I got a new attitude and went to the soaking class. People were coming into the meeting room with pillows and blankets. I saw one lady dressed in what looked like her pajamas. But with further investigation, it was just one ugly dress. I figured I had to behave and be a good little boy.

Well, the teaching was OK. Then we had a prayer and they put on some Indian flute, smoke-a-joint music. I found a place in the corner and laid down to soak. Why don't they call it marinating or pickling, or being in His presence? We called it "sloaking" because it was OK to sleep or meditate. As I got into the presence of God, I heard Him ask this question, "Why are you so angry with your father?" I cried out, "Because he tried to take credit for my spiritual success, and he isn't spiritual enough to recognize what You promised me in a vision in 1996." In that vision, I saw my mother at 14 years old walking up a hill praying about a coming revival when the Glory falls and masses of people are saved and healed. "You promised me a Harley and a Rolex watch as gifts to be signs of this coming move of Your Spirit. You said that you would give them to me as signs of the timing of this revival," I reminded Him.

I continued to argue with God. "That very Rolex was the same watch that Leif Hetland wears, and he was the one who connected me with Jack Taylor. I have never been able to please my dad when it is a spiritual matter, but when I have a little success, he takes credit for it.

He doesn't even know that the mantle of the prophet that I walk in was from Grandpa. If Dad had been willing to pay the price, he could have been a giant in the faith. When it comes to spiritual things, he doesn't have a clue. I believe he's ashamed of me, and now he's trying to take credit for it." I found myself, lying on the floor, very upset!

My internal conversation with God resumed. "You promised seven years ago that Jack Taylor would be a spiritual father to me before I was released into my ministry. How could my father try to take credit for that, just because he prayed some "namby, pamby" prayer? If he had been the man of God he was supposed to be, I would not have needed Jack Taylor. It has been my obedience to You, which brought Jack Taylor into my life....it makes me mad that after all these years he is trying to take the credit."

The Holy Spirit spoke sternly, *"Even after last night's validation in Sonship, you still think like an orphan."* He went on, "Charlie, if I had wanted Moses to be the only one delivered from Egypt, I would have never hardened Pharaoh's heart ten times. I wanted to deliver Moses and the whole nation. That's why I hardened all these men's hearts against you. They weren't capable of spiritually fathering you. I would not allow them access to that area in your life." "Even my father?" I asked. "Yes, even your father," was the reply. "But why Lord?" I inquired, as I approached a new level of brokenness I had not experienced before. Then He gently explained, "If I had allowed them to father you, they would have molded you into their image, and not Mine. Therefore, I left you an orphan till this season, to bring healing and deliverance to the spiritually fatherless in this nation."

Next, I saw a vision of a list with my dad's name, and the names of nine other leaders, to whom I had submitted, on it. The Holy Spirit told me to let go of my bitterness and anger because the men had been held back by God, and weren't capable of fathering me in the spirit in this last season. As I started repenting for my resentments and anger, the Lord started speaking to me about those who are hurting, and how much they need deliverance and healing from the *orphan spirit.*

The Lord then asked me if I was up to the task of bringing healing to the body of Christ in this area. As I answered the call, I saw a vision of a gym full of boxers in training. There were two boxers sparring in the ring. Others were working out all over at different exercise stations. Some were working the speed bag, some were hitting the heavy bag, and others were jumping rope. As I looked on the wall, I saw a poster of an upcoming main event. It read: **Church Fathers vs. Kingdom Sons, Are You Ready to Rumble?** The cover of this book represents the scene I saw in that vision.

This book is the sharing of my heart and the challenge to seek change for the multitude of church-going people, who like me, love the Lord, but have not experienced all that the Father has for them. There is a greater spiritual experience to be discovered and it is my hope, passion and mission to know for myself all that it means to be a son of God and to share that message with all who will listen. This book is dedicated to spiritual orphans who are becoming Kingdom Sons.

Charles Coker, Jr.

Some men in this book have served as mentors to me, yet were not spiritual fathers. Those men will be noted by an asterisk*.

Personal Authority

Round One

Why My Father!

I heard myself say, "Lord, I'm still feeling raw and a little angry on the inside about You hardening the hearts of all these leaders that I had submitted to in ministry." At least the hardening of these men's hearts explains why the relationships only went so far. "But God, it's not fair!" continued to resound in my head. I seemed to hear the Father respond, "Well son, tell me what was fair about the cross on which they crucified My Son?" I understand God's mercy and grace, but it still doesn't feel fair!

I was starting to get the meaning of the word my mother gave me on her deathbed. My mother called me to her side three weeks before she died in 1997. I remember the call at the office. She asked me to drive to Sarasota, where she was going to have heart surgery in a few days. She told me that she wanted to see me alone, and to come in the morning. After I hung up the phone, I went into a vision. I saw my father as the head of the family, and that all four of us kids were under his blessing. Then I saw the patriarchal position of my father being lowered as I was being promoted to that position. I asked the Lord, "What does this mean?" He said, "There is an authority shift coming to your family." I didn't see my mother in the vision and asked the Lord, "Is it her time?" I asked if my father was going to die, also. God told me, "No, he isn't." I asked, "How can I walk in this position of patriarch while my father is still alive?" The Lord told me that this would only work within the realm of the Kingdom of God and in surrendered vessels. The next day, I went to see Mom, and she began the conversation.

"Charlie, I took a walk with Jesus the other night," she began. "We were walking in heaven. We stopped and looked over a balcony, and He showed me your life. I know who you are, and I saw your calling." She continued, "Your father is a good man, and a man of faith, but not a man of the Spirit (Kingdom). If you let him, he will destroy the gift of God that is on your life. This is your test, not his, but when you prove to him it's from God, he will serve you." She went on, "Listen to me carefully; if you fail this test, God will not use you in the ministry you have been called to fulfill." Then she finished, "You must learn to do war with honor, or you will fail."

My mother had surgery a few days later, and then suffered a stroke that left her without the ability to speak. During the next three weeks of recovery, she never spoke a clear word to us. The doctors released her to travel across the state to Vero Beach, Florida, to a rehab hospital. I let my sister use my Lincoln Town Car so the ride would be more comfortable for her, and I drove to Vero to meet them. I was standing on the street corner waiting, and my mother, who had not spoken a clear word during the past three weeks, saw me standing on the sidewalk. She looked at my sister, and clear as a bell said, "That boy is going to be a fat preacher. Tell him no one listens to a fat preacher, and tell him I said to lose some weight!" My sister was shocked to hear her speak. We all thought that it was funny, and now we have yet another family story to tell about Mom. My mother died the next day.

The journey God has had me take has been about learning to stop thinking and acting like an orphan, and to start thinking like a Son and manifest the Kingdom. I have said more than once to the Lord, "Lord, my journey has been hard! I know that You said, 'No,' years ago when I asked for a spiritual father. You had that lady give me scripture about the anointing that would teach me all things. She said the Father wanted me to know the real meaning of 1 John 2:27:

> *But the anointing which you have received from Him abides in you, and you do not need that anyone teach you; but as the same anointing teaches you concerning all things, and is true, and is not a lie, and just as it has taught you, you will abide in Him.*

In conjunction with this, the Father told me that He would not allow others to make it easy on me. He revealed to me that the day would come when He would send people, who if they listened, would learn from my teachings. What took me years, they would do in months, what took me months, they would do in weeks, and what took me weeks, they would do in days. The power of my blessing would be an impartation of grace in their lives, and they would receive it from the Lord when I lay my hands on them.

Still this question nagged at me, "But my father!* Why did you list him with all of those leaders that you had me submit to in ministry?" Dad was never a pastor. He was always a deacon, Sunday school teacher, and song leader, while Mom played the piano. My Dad was a good father in the natural, but wasn't a man of the Spirit. He was incapable of fulfilling the role of my spiritual father in the Kingdom. He was only able to be my mentor.

I remember that when there was a major problem in the church, Dad and my four spiritual uncles (deacons) would have meetings at the church. Within a few weeks, the pastor would resign or the board would call a membership meeting, and the whole church would have what they called a vote of confidence. Sometimes the pastor would stay, and other times he would leave.

I learned that a man's true character is revealed in the dark when no one else is watching but God. I saw this with my father late one night when I came into the living room to find him praying. I just stood still, and listened to him pray. He asked God to help him do what was right. He was willing to keep his opinions to himself, but needed help doing what was right. This unguarded moment of my Dad's life has always had an impact on me, yet he didn't even know I was there. My father always tried to make righteous stands, even if it cost him.

Spiritual leadership should start in the home. My father was a leader in the Church and lived by those rules. He governed his home with the same iron hand that the church used. Yes, there were rules but there was always a loving side, too.

I have to admit that I have a strong personality, and God needed to deal with my rebellion. I was raised in the church, so I was saved at a very young age. I will share more of my early life later. I remember taking a walk with my Dad when I was nineteen years old and at a crossroad in my life. We talked about the bleeding ulcers that I had developed and how I wanted to join the Army. I had fathered a child and denied that he was mine. I was lying about the girl and running from God. That girl is now my wife of 33 years. (She won; her prayers worked!) Instead of calling the police and having me arrested for date rape, she started praying. Her mom and my mom were praying together, and I was under so much conviction that I suffered from those bleeding ulcers. I let my father know that the doctor was going to put me on a baby food diet, and if the bleeding didn't stop, they were going to have to operate. Dad looked at me and spoke flat-out, **"It's not what you're eating, Son, it's what's eating you."** After letting that sink in for a minute, Dad went on, "If you run from responsibility, you will be running for the rest of your life." At that precise moment, the Holy Spirit came on me, and I repented and asked Jesus to cleanse my heart. I immediately went, made it right with Susie, and within six months we were married.

We started off strong in the church as a new family, and all was well, until we had a conflict at church. The youth pastor was having an affair. My cousin felt like the leadership of the church had wronged him. So I took up an offense for my cousin. I used it as an excuse to leave the church and all of that "church politics" garbage. We lasted as a church-going family for about three years before I gradually became a reprobate. At the same time, I was becoming successful in business. God chose this occasion to allow other spiritual wounds—from being held at knife-point and sexually abused at 7 years old—to start coming to the surface.

A deacon's seventeen-year-old son, who later killed two women and died on death row, abused me. Because of the unhealed wounds, I became addicted to pornography, and was committing adultery. Alcohol was starting to control areas of my life, too. Basically, my life was coming apart at the seams.

My mother came to my business one day and said that she wanted to talk to my checkbook. She began to tell my checkbook that its owner was a sinful man, and there was a call of God on his life. She looked at me and said, "Every day of your life I have prayed that the blessings of God would overtake you. I have prayed in every dime and every dollar you have made, but you have turned your heart from God. He has promised me that you would fulfill your calling. Today, I made a deal with God. I gave God permission to do what ever it takes for you to get into heaven. He could even kill you, if need be, because you're an adulterer, you're addicted to pornography, and a cheat." She pointed at me and added, "You are a liar; you are not worthy to be a husband or a father." She gave me a strong look and told me I had better repent and get right with God. Then she closed the office door and left. About two minutes later, she came back in and said, "By the way, I love Jesus more than I love you. I will see you in heaven. You can make it easy, or you can make it hard. The choice is yours to make." You would think that such a talking-to would have gotten my attention, but I only hardened my heart more.

The wife, who had prayed for me and believed God's promises for me as well, was starting to have her own spiritual crisis. The pornography and the wounds of being date raped by me were an open door for the enemy to take her out. She started having her own relationships outside our marriage. We were on a downward spiral. We both had been raised in the church and both knew the truth about God and His ways. Sin has a way of taking you further than you wanted to go, keeping you longer than you wanted to stay, making you do what you swore you would never do, and making you pay more than you wanted to pay.

In my life there has been a patten of three-and-one-half year cycles of spiritual trials. Some I have passed, and some I have had to retake later. At the three-year mark of marriage, we failed the test and left the church system. Then seven years later, two, three-and-one-half year cycles later, my mother spoke judgment over me. Later, my wife of thirteen years moved out, and we were heading for divorce. She was so hurt and wounded that she left both boys with me. I was at the end of my rope.

On August 30, 1993 at two thirty in the morning, I knelt down beside my pool table and prayed this prayer: "God, if you are the God of my mother, a supernatural God, if You're that God, the one who she says has the power to change a man's heart, if You are that God, I will give You a chance to change me. I will not make promises any more without a change in my heart, because I am a liar, a thief, and a whoremonger. I am evil to the core of my heart, and if You can't change my heart, I will never be able to serve You."

As I stood up, I waited for God to say or do something. "Boy," I said, "That was the most honest prayer I have ever prayed." As I started to leave the room, suddenly lightning went off in the room. It was the brightest light I had ever seen! Out from the light walked Jesus. He had eyes that pierced my soul. He held out His hand and started to move in my direction. As He stretched his hand to me, He said, "Charlie, tonight you choose who you will serve! If you put your hand in My hand, I will never leave you or forsake you. But if you don't choose Me," He pointed and said, "I will let hell have its way with you." As He pointed, I saw hell open up, I heard the screams, the smell of sulfur, and I was petrified with fear. At that moment in time, I surrendered 100% to the Lord Jesus Christ. He had become my King, Lord, and Savior. Like I had a choice! Sweet little baby Jesus in the manger had grown up and was going to let hell have its way with me. My reality check had just bounced. I had met the King of the Kingdom!

I have always understood the blood covenant that Jesus made on the cross, but my personal relationship with God took on a different reality. He had intentions of shedding my blood, if I didn't obey Him! Several years later, I asked Jesus why He manifested to me that night. I thought I was something special and waited for the answer. He told me it had little to do with me. He said, "I had your mother in my face, day and night holding me accountable for the promises I made to her about you. That's what moved me to visit you."

In our conversation Jesus asked me if He could use me to bring change to His church. I started to argue that I didn't like His church—it's filled with hypocrites. I pleaded with Him, "Please, I have fallen in love with You. I see a King who has a Kingdom that is bigger than the ugly church system. Please don't make me go there. They have hurt me, and they are mean." He then said, "Charlie, you're talking about my bride." He continued on, "You can't bring change by standing on the outside taking pot-shots at My church. You have to be on the inside to bring change." Jesus said that He was going to bring me to a place of maturity. In that maturity, I could rebel against the church system I was told to submit to, and still walk in LOVE. "THIS will bring the change from church to Kingdom. Follow my example in my Word. I was part of the religious system of My day. It is time to release present day truth for all to change." This experience with Christ was the beginning of Church Fathers versus Kingdom Sons for me. As the rumbling started, so did the miracles, and the Kingdom was advancing as the King was revealed.

That same night Jesus showed me two visions: one presenting twenty couples in a marriage ceremony with Susie and me among them; the other was of me on stage speaking to thousands, sharing the goodness of my God and preaching the gospel. It took God eleven months to fulfill these two visions. These visions helped me have faith to believe God was going to heal my marriage and my life, so they were important keys to Susie's and my marriage restoration.

Many people ask the question, "How long have you been saved?" Most of the time, I say August 30, 1993, but the truth is that I had given my heart to Jesus at about five years old. At the age of nine, I had a visitation from the Lord and received the baptism of the Holy Spirit. In this encounter I saw that I was going to preach to masses of black people. As a result I had always concluded that I was going to be a missionary to Africa.

We had a missionary from Africa visit the church, and when he asked for commitments, I went to the front for prayer about going to the mission field. Truth be known, I felt I was born again and had eternal life. Even though I was a racist and was a reprobate in many other areas of my life, God had a plan and was not going to let me wiggle out of His hands. I have long identified with Nicodemus.

There was a man of the Pharisees, named Nicodemus, a ruler of the Jews: The same came to Jesus by night, and said unto him, Rabbi, we know that thou art a teacher come from God: for no man can do these miracles that thou doest, except God be with him. Jesus answered and said unto him, Verily, verily, I say unto thee, except a man be born again, <u>he cannot see the kingdom of God</u>. (John 3: 1-3: KJV)

Nicodemus was a leader of the religious church of His day. He came to Jesus and affirmed that God was with Him by the miracles that followed Him. Nicodemus was asking, "What must I do to have the same thing You have?" It is all about a King, who lives in the Spirit realm, and His kingdom. I believe that I was born again, but was unwilling to pay the price to enter the kingdom realm that I live in today. I feel there are many leaders in the church who love God and are born-again, but have only been able to see the Kingdom and are unwilling to enter into it. Therefore, we have many orphan CEOs as leaders in the church today.

That night in 1993, the King of the Kingdom of Heaven captured my complete heart, and I entered into the Kingdom. On that extraordinary night, I called my Dad and asked if he would bring me a Bible. I was so ashamed that I could not find a Bible in my house to wake up with the next morning. He showed up at about 4:00 a.m. I asked him if he would drop off a duffel bag full of pornography at the dump on his way home. He began to understand that something had changed in me that night!

Three days later, I was working at one of our rental houses. The tenant had moved out, and I was checking on it to get it ready for the next tenant. He had left some alcohol in the bottom cabinet of the kitchen. While I was cleaning it out, a very large ruling-level demon attacked me physically. This demon was huge! It started off as very beautiful. At first I thought it was from God, but when I shouted the name, "Jesus," this thing started hitting me and trying to kill me! I took the alcohol out on the back porch and started breaking the bottles in a recycling bin. This demonic thing was still trying to kill me! I started screaming at the top of my lungs, "Jesus, Jesus, the blood of Jesus is against you. Satan, the blood of Jesus rebukes you." I remembered a childhood Bible story where the demons were cast out of a man and into the pigs. The pigs ran into the water and drowned. I figured out that demons couldn't swim, so I jumped into the swimming pool. Each time I would go under the water, the torment would subside, and I could think and pray. I would come up for air and rebuke the devil.

To make a long story short, the cops came and they took me to the hospital. They had me strapped down to the gurney and were asking me questions about this demon I saw. I was arguing about the big old demon that was trying to kill me. Then I heard the voice of my King say, "Charlie, settle down it's going to be OK. I am with you! It's going to be OK." Peace like a river flooded my emotions, and the Holy Spirit started giving me the words to say, to answer the questions that the doctors were asking.

After a few hours, my father came to see me. As he stood at the foot of the bed, he started to tell me that he wanted me to sign some papers that would voluntarily Baker Act me. The Baker Act is a commitment to a mental health facility, done either voluntarily or by legal action. As he asked me to sign the papers, I started to explain that it was only a demon. I had proclaimed the name of Jesus, pleaded the pure sinless blood of Christ, and the demon had to flee. I started to argue with him. He explained that voluntarily signing the papers would be better than if they had to force me to go to a mental institution.

I looked at him and said, "Dad, just take me home to your house and every thing will be all right." He still would not give in to my way of thinking, and I was starting to get angry with him. Then I heard the words of my new King. "FOR ONCE IN YOUR LIFE, DO WHAT YOUR AUTHORITY TELLS YOU TO DO, AND DO IT WITH THE RIGHT ATTITUDE!"

This was God telling me that throughout my whole life I had never submitted to authority. He said, "For once in your life…" I was thirty-three years old and was still dealing with rebellion.

I looked at my father and said, "Dad, I think you're wrong in what you have asked me to do, but because you are my authority, I will do it. Sorry for the attitude. Please forgive me." At the very moment the word forgive came out of my mouth, the Holy Spirit reached into my heart and ripped rebellion out of me. I felt it come out of my soul and my spirit. This was the beginning of my deliverances from the demonic spirits that I had allowed into my life. At that very moment, the Lord started speaking to me about His plans for my life. He began to show me that submitting to authority was an absolute MUST in order to be successful in life and ministry.

Within seven days the Lord had brought much healing and deliverance. He dealt with my rebellion to my father and started to rebuild me as a man, so He could trust me with my wife.

My father was the first spiritual authority that I had to submit to. That was the first Kingdom principle God showed me. The second important Kingdom principle God showed me was that authority must start first with me, then with my family. I had just had a heart change and fallen in love with Susie like never before, but, we had lived a lifestyle that was ungodly, to say the least.

Susie was having relationships outside of our marriage that were hurting me, and the enemy was still influencing me. One night I made a plan and borrowed a friend's car. I walked a few blocks from the beach and at 1:30 in the morning was sitting outside the window of the house where Susie and her date were doing the nasty. I sat with a .44 Magnum and was planning to scare this guy away from my wife, and if necessary, kill him.

As I waited outside the house where my wife and her date were, I heard the voice of my new King. He said, "It is your fault that she is sleeping with this man. I do not hold this sin against her; I hold it against you. This is your fault." I thought, "How could this be? She is inside this guy's house, and it's my fault?"

I knew this voice was the voice of my new King, so I left and returned home to pray. I asked the Lord, "How can this be my fault? Your word is very clear, and what she is doing is sin. If this is my fault, can you prove it in Scripture?" The Lord replied, "Glad you asked. Go to Hosea 4:6: *My people are destroyed for lack of knowledge. Because you have rejected knowledge, I also will reject you from being priest for Me; because you have forgotten the law of your God, I also will forget your children."*

This verse jumped off the page at me. The Lord spoke to me again saying, "If you're going to be a priest for me, I will give you knowledge on how to bring the proper sacrifice that I require in every arena of authority where I will put you. The man is the priest of his home. Follow my principles, and I will help you recover not only your wife, but also your children."

I read on in Hosea, Chapter 4, where verses 12-14 leapt off the page at me:

> *...people ask counsel at their stocks, and their staff declareth unto them: for the spirit of whoredoms hath caused them to err, and they have gone a whoring from under their God. They sacrifice upon the tops of the mountains, and burn incense upon the hills, under oaks and poplars and elms, because the shadow thereof is good: therefore your daughters shall commit whoredom, and your spouses shall commit adultery. I will not punish your daughters when they commit whoredom, nor your spouses when they commit adultery: for "the men" themselves are separated with whores, and they sacrifice with harlots: therefore the people that doth not understand shall fall. (KJV)*

Now, convinced with this Scripture I asked, "What do I do?" The Holy Spirit started giving me words to pray. I understood for the first time that I was responsible for the condition of my marriage and my home! Therefore, I stood in my place of authority, and repented for my sins and the sins that my wife was committing. That night I started to walk in the authority of the Kingdom with my new King.

I remember a talk with my father when he told me that my wife was making a mockery of me and I needed to get real about my marriage. "It's over son. You're going to have to face the reality that she doesn't want to be married to you," he told me.

I told my father, "I understand why you are saying what you're saying, but God promised to restore my marriage. He called her a godly woman, full of faith, and He is going to heal her from the inside-out. If you can't believe that God can and will heal my marriage, and walk with me, I will never talk about it with you again." My father looked at me and said, "OK, I will believe with you."

This was a very hard time for me personally, but very much needed training for the reigning and ruling He was trying to teach me. If you can't rule yourself, you will be disqualified from rule in other areas. Susie had moved out, and I was trying to live a holy lifestyle. Remembering the years of pornography and sexual addition were driving me crazy.

One night I was in the shower and had to start praying for some help. A demonic oppression came over me, and I felt hornier than a three balled billie goat. This made me cry out to my new King for help. The Holy Spirit told me, "I cannot help you with your problem, because it was your actions that put this area out of balance." He continued, "Until you surrender the sexual part of your life to Me completely, and offer it to Me as a sacrifice, I will not help You." So I knelt down and made a personal altar in the shower. I presented that sexual part of my life completely to the Lordship of Jesus Christ. The pressure was replaced with peace and power, and I felt His presence at a greater level.

Kingdom Key:
When His presence becomes more valuable than my pleasure, I will walk in peace and power!

I walked out of the shower and was drying off, when Jesus walked into the room. He had a robe in His hand. He said, "Because you have chosen to walk in holiness, you will need My robe of righteousness to wear." He put a beautiful white robe around me and gave me instructions to write this quote on a 3x5 card and read it every day till my mind was renewed. So I started every day for years with *"Charles L. Coker Jr is as righteous as Jesus Christ is, because He gave me His robe to wear. I can do what He did and greater."*

Kingdom Key:
Righteousness is a gift from Jesus!
Holiness is a choice that empowers righteousness.

After God showed me that He was going to heal my marriage, I had a come-to-Jesus-meeting with Him about my weaknesses in the sexual area of my life. I had truly fallen in love with Susie again, but I had to be honest; whether it was six months or five years, I was afraid that I would cheat on her and hurt her again. I told Jesus that I wanted Him to release Susie from the marriage, so she could find a good husband who would not cheat on her.

After three days of talking to the Lord about this, He came to me and asked one more time if cheating was truly the only fear that I had about my marriage. He asked me, "If I guarantee that you will never touch another woman inappropriately, do you want Me to heal your marriage?" I asked, "Could you do that?" He said, "I am God. Yes, I can!" I told God, if He could make that guarantee to me, I wanted my marriage restored. He then told me to stand on my Bible. As I literally stood with my feet on my Bible, He audibly spoke these words: "Charles Layton Coker, Jr., if you ever touch another woman (in an inappropriate way), I will KILL you stone dead!" He took care of that little lust problem in short order!

Susie and I are writing another book, "*From Rape to Righteousness, Redeeming the Bride of Christ,*" that will get into more detail about how God healed Susie and me in this area of our lives.

The lessons I have learned can be found in Galatians 4:1-7:

Now I say that the heir, as long as he is a child, does not differ at all from a slave, though he is master of all, but is under guardians and stewards until the time appointed by the father.

Over the next few years God taught me how to submit to authority. This Kingdom revelation continues living inside of me.

Kingdom Keys:

1. The Kingdom operates under authority.

2. The King (Jesus) was under authority until the appointed time. (Galatians 4:1-7).

3. The Kingdom has different levels of authority.

4. When His presence becomes more valuable than my pleasure, I will walk in peace and power!

5. Righteousness is a gift from Jesus! Holiness is a choice that empowers righteousness.

Round 2

The Place of My Birth

And He has made from one blood every nation of men to dwell on all the face of the earth, and has determined their preappointed times and the boundaries of their dwelling… (Acts 17:26)

I was puzzled about why Pastor Buddy* of Central Assembly was one of the leaders whose heart God had hardened so much that he was unable to father me. I was only submitted to him for about 6 weeks. I would find out why years later.

After the incredible life changing experience of having Jesus tell me to follow Him, or He was going to let hell have its way with me, coupled with the revelation that He loved me enough to put my natural life on the line; the Lord showed me that His judgment was one of both love and mercy, not wrath or death. The purpose of His call to me was to LIVE and LOVE.

He knew what it would take to complete that task! The supernatural power of God changed my heart of stone into a heart of flesh. The supernatural was a demand for change, and it was the only way I could have followed Him. I believe the power of the supernatural is the key to a revival being sustained that will change the culture of our nation.

When a friend tells you to go to hell, it only hurts, but when Jesus, the one who holds life and death in His hands, tells you to go to hell; that's a different story. Jesus certainly had this redneck's attention.

The fear of the Lord is the beginning of wisdom: a good understanding have all they that do his commandments: his praise endureth forever. (Psalm 111:10 KJV)

Jesus began to speak to me about getting involved with the local church. He said that I couldn't bring change by shooting from the outside, but only by being involved. One of my life long friends, Tim Bishop, who was instrumental in my conversion, was attending Central Assembly. Tim and I were friends all through high school, so you know we got into a lot of trouble—car-racing and girl-chasing to name just a few of our sports.

Tim got saved about a year before I had my encounter with Jesus. He worked for UPS and would eat lunch in my office at the lighting store. So, I had to hear about his new life with Jesus almost everyday. Tim was not from a religious family; so all this Jesus stuff was fresh to him. After about eight months of him witnessing to me, he started pushing my buttons and asking questions like, "Charlie, how can a person who was raised in church like you, ignore the truth, and live the way you're living?" The smoke would roll out of my ears.

With my church background, I gave him an earful, and I started hating him with a demonic passion. Tim lived in my neighborhood and as my family and I would be taking the boat out on Sunday morning, we would pass by his house as his nice little Christian family prepared to go to church. We would just ignore them and not even wave. I found out later that Tim was also my father's UPS driver, and he would stop and have prayer with my dad before he would come have lunch at my office. Tim would tell Dad, "Mr. Coker, he hates me!" Then my father would say, "No it's the Holy Spirit in you that he hates. Tim, you are the only one who can speak to his life, don't stop now." Tim ate lunch at my store for many months and was faithful to be a light, even when I didn't like it.

On the afternoon after I had my encounter and deliverance with Jesus, Tim's son, Mike, came down to the house to play pool with my boys. I had found a bottle of alcohol that I had missed the night before and was pouring it out into sink when Mike walked in. I told Mike, "You can take money and buy this stuff, and because you buy it, you think you own it. But if gone unchecked for very long, it will own YOU. Be careful. Jesus came into my life last night and set me free."

Mike ran home and started telling his father, "Dad, something has happened to Mr. Coker."

Tim and I rekindled our friendship. We started walking the neighborhood and praying every night, believing that God was going to answer His promise of healing my marriage. Meanwhile, Tim's wife was glad Susie had left me. Sometimes women don't forgive very fast. They also stick together as thick as thieves, but it wasn't long before she saw the changes on the inside of me and was won back over to my side. This is another lesson I was beginning to learn that I will discuss more in the coming pages.

My friend, Tim, went to the largest Pentecostal church in town, and his pastor, Buddy, was one of those men in my life blocked by God from fathering me. He was the most surprising of all the leaders on the list. You see, he was the pastor of Central Assembly of God, a church formed in 1965 by splitting away from First Assembly of God, where my father and four uncles were on the board of leadership. The board had one of those votes of confidence, and the pastor left with part of the congregation, despite the board's approval of his leadership. The founding pastor, apparently, was a man who had a vision from God about his calling to the city; nevertheless, Central was started out of an act of rebellion. (That's what I've been taught about church splits.) I don't want to throw my father and all my uncles under the bus, but I feel that the cloud of God's favor had moved. I believe that my father and uncles missed it, because they stayed at First Assembly. If they had been kingdom thinkers, they would have joined that place of blessing. There is no comparison between the fruitfulness of blessings from Him rather than the approval of a board of men...religious or not. If Central closed her doors today, the impact would be felt all over the city. If the church that my father helped to start closed, very few would even notice. The city would have no void. The effectiveness of the church I was raised in doesn't compare to Central. (This is my opinion only.) All the board members are dead except my father, and I can out run him. (Maybe)

Since Central started from a split, I was hesitant to go there. Sometimes we think our kids don't know what's going on, but kids pick up offenses that parents have or had. I remember when families left our church and how it was discussed. Yes, it gets into our spirits, and we make judgments in our hearts even when we shouldn't. **Kingdom thinking can remove such things from our hearts.**

Since my father was my new spiritual authority, I asked his permission to worship at Central. Tim was very involved there. It was the happening place in town. Dad had no problem with me going and was very supportive. He was very pleased that it was a Pentecostal church. He told me that I didn't have to go to his church but to go where God sent me.

I went to lunch with the pastor, Buddy, and told him that I wanted to attend Central. I told him that my father had given his approval. Pastor Buddy told me it was important to get plugged in with a home group and serve. The church had a full time Christian counselor on staff. This was important, because Susie and I were really going to need counseling.

Susie moved back home. I was starting to be the spiritual leader of in our house, but she didn't like this church. Firmly, I put my foot down and said, "As the spiritual head of this home, if you're going to live in this house, you will go to church on Sundays." She told me in short order where to go. I pushed the issue, and she said, "Fine." The next Sunday we all got up and headed off to church. As I was getting into my car, she got into her car and went to a different church. I got so mad! The Lord said, "Pick your battles next time, and be more specific!"

The Lord showed me Ephesians 5, where it says:

Wives, submit to your own husbands, as to the Lord. For the husband is head of the wife, as also Christ is head of the church; and He is the Savior of the body. Therefore, just as the church is subject to Christ, so let the wives be to their own husbands in everything. Husbands, love your wives, just as Christ also loved the church and gave Himself for her, that He might sanctify and cleanse her with the washing of water by the word... (Ephesians 5:22-25)

Kingdom Key:
Until you are willing to die for your wife, you will always want to kill her.

The church counselor had a few sessions with me, and some with Susie. After a few weeks, he got both of us together and said the most shocking thing I have ever heard. This Christian counselor said, "Susie doesn't want to be married to you." He said, "With your history, and Biblically, because of adultery on both sides, God would permit a divorce." He was quoting Mark 10:4:4-5 (KJV), *"And they said, Moses suffered to write a bill of divorcement, and to put her away. And Jesus answered and said unto them, For the hardness of your heart he wrote you this precept."*

The church has used this scripture to justify divorce, and in many cases it may be unavoidable and the right thing to do. In my case, the King of the Kingdom was showing me He would heal my marriage, if I would let Him take my heart of stone and turn it into a heart of flesh.

The counselor then said, "I don't think your marriage has any hope of making it." God had made me a promise. No Christian counselor or even my wife can change a promise from God. Take a look at the passage, and you will see the reason that the church system has as high a divorce rate as the world. The hardness of the hearts is the root cause of divorce.

Three weeks after I had my encounter with Jesus, I was sitting in church when our town sports hero walked down the aisle and gave his heart back to the Lord. He played for three championship seasons with the Miami Hurricanes, and then played for the New York Jets. While he was down at the altar, I heard the Lord say, "I want you to go welcome your new brother into the Kingdom." I was not going to do that. I said, "Lord you know that isn't my brother, he's black." He was a 6-foot-1-inch black man, who drove a white Lexus and had a white wife. No way on God's green earth was I going to be nice to him! "He can't be my brother: he is a n_!" I thought in my heart. God tried to speak to me about this, but I walked out of the church that morning.

The next morning I got up at 5:30 a.m. to read my Bible. When I had my encounter with God, I asked Him, "How can I know You better?" The Lord said, "By reading My Word." This was a problem because I didn't read well. As I opened the Bible, the first page I turned to was John 14:26: *"But the Helper, the Holy Spirit, whom the Father will send in*

My name, He will teach you all things, and bring to your remembrance all things that I said to you." I began reading the Bible for the first time in over 10 years, and I discovered that the Holy Spirit was my teacher. I had a hard time learning to read in school, and I read only on a third grade level. I prayed that first day after my encounter with the Lord, asking the Holy Spirit to teach me to read. The Lord spoke to me and said if I would give Him one hour in the morning everyday, He would teach me to read. To make a long story short, He directed me to use a King James giant print Bible with no commentary to learn to read. I asked Him why there was no commentary in this Bible. The Lord said He was the author, and He could tell me what the meaning was if I had questions.

As I got up to do my reading that next morning after storming out of church, my King reminded me about my sin problem with black people. I felt His conviction but refused to deal with it. The next morning the same thing happened. For six days in a row I felt the same conviction. On the seventh day at 5:30 a.m., I opened my giant print, red-letter Bible, and, because of my stubbornness and my confused little mind, all 1,987 pages of it were blank. Yes, blank, pure white blank pages front to back. I asked the Lord what was going on. He spoke with a stern voice and he said, "Today, you make a choice of keeping your sin of racism or having a relationship with me." I told him that I didn't know how to fix it. He asked me, "What did you do about your sin when I first came to you, after you knelt down by your pool table?" I said, "I confessed it as sin and asked You to forgive me." "The sin I just showed you in your heart this morning can be washed white as snow with the same prayer," He said. So, I asked the Lord to forgive me of the sin of racism that very morning. I spoke quietly, "I don't know how it got there, but if it doesn't please You, take it away."

The Lord asked me to start praying every day for this couple I refused to befriend and encourage, because the husband was black. My first prayer may not be exciting to you, but it was to God that day; He knows my heart. Old habits take time to change, and the Lord was gracious with me. It went like this, "Dear Jesus, bless that n_ and his white wife. Please help them to walk with You." In the Kingdom, there is always grace to grow. The printing returned to the pages of my Bible, and the King of my heart was very pleased with me.

As I look back, my stay at Central was very short, but I was exposed to a lot of the ministry I walk in today. The apostolic, prophetic, and my true passion, to heal racism in the body of Christ, are what this church exposed me to. Pastor Buddy was very loving and helpful, but it became apparent that God had a different fellowship for my family. He blessed me when I came and told him that God was moving my family to a Baptist church in town. It was my decision to leave. I can see that while God put me at Central for only about six weeks, much happened in that short time. This was the first time I had been exposed to the prophetic, and this pastor is an Apostle.

In 1993, the apostolic was just starting to be released into the body of Christ. It has been great reflecting back and seeing the different anointings and callings working according to Ephesians 4: 11-13:

And He Himself gave some to be apostles, some prophets, some evangelists, and some pastors and teachers, for the equipping of the saints for the work of ministry, for the edifying of the body of Christ, till we all come to the unity of the faith and of the knowledge of the Son of God, to a perfect man, to the measure of the stature of the fullness of Christ…

This short time was very enlightening, showing my calling and personal inheritance from God. I didn't know, then, what God was doing, but He was starting to train me to see the Kingdom and rule with Kingdom principles, all the while submitting to the church systems.

Kingdom Keys

1. Holy Fear of the King and His Kingdom is helpful for gaining wisdom and understanding.

2. The King can set you free from whatever has you in bondage.

3. Kingdom thinking will unite and not divide.

4. Kingdom is a generational view of where we came from and where we are going.

5. Kingdom principles don't work well with a hard heart.

6. The King of the Kingdom will not tolerate racism.

7. Until you're willing to die for your spouse, you will want to kill him/her.

Round 3

Living for Jesus, Baptist Style

As the Lord was starting to move in my heart to look for a different church, I was becoming irritated in my spirit and could not figure out why.

Kingdom Key:
When your peace has left, you're not right.

The Kingdom works within a smaller gate of tolerance when it comes to relationships. If you have an issue with your brother, go make it right. The Kingdom lifestyle that Jesus was teaching me was a lifestyle of repentance. One day the Lord began to teach me about false accusations. He asked how badly I wanted to be like Him. I said that I was willing to change as fast as I could to His image. He gave me a principle to live by.

"Charlie, every false accusation has enough truth to apply personally; you can use that truth to become more like Me, but it requires a spirit of repentance and humility."

Well, the Lord told me to go see Tommy, another old friend of mine. We had grown up together, and I was supposed to let him know that I had given my heart to the Lord. Tommy had gotten saved and was a deacon in a Baptist church in Winter Beach, Florida. The year before, we had gone hunting together in Missouri. On the trip he witnessed to me, like my friend Tim had. I was in no frame of mind to hear about God, and I had a rifle in my hand.

I went to Tommy's door, and I knocked. Tommy came to the door with a look of surprise on his face. As I told him about my conversion, he started to tear up. He said, "Last week the Lord told me to give you a call but I didn't." "So why didn't you?" I asked. He spoke further, "Last time I tried to tell you about Jesus, you threatened to shoot me. Remember?" I retorted, "I got saved." As we talked, Tommy started telling me about a course for new believers at the Baptist church called "Survival Kit." As he continued on, I was feeling like the Lord was telling me to commit to the course. I normally would not have done it, because I am Pentecostal, and we don't believe the same way as Baptists do. I gave in and told Tommy I would pray about it.

"I will pray about it" has become a standard answer among Christians which really means, "Heck no! I am not going to do that." But, I knew it was my King telling me to commit. I had dealt with many things in my life the last few weeks and was in NO mood to deal with religious Baptists, who believed that once saved, always saved, and don't believe in divine healing, and don't speak in tongues. No way was I going to let a religious spirit stop my progress in coming to spiritual maturity!

About a week later Tommy's sister, a friend of Susie's, came by the house to pick something up. She had heard that I had become a Christian and was happy for me. She stated, "You know, Charlie, I am taking a course at my brother's church for new believers called "Survival Kit." You should come and learn how to survive this new life in Christ." I did it again… "Leeann, I will 'pray about it'." As she left, I felt like I had grieved the Holy Spirit, but I was not going to talk about it. I was not going to go to a Baptist church!

I was becoming very agitated in my spirit, and I understood why. I knew this is what grieving the Spirit felt like. My new King was not pleased with me, and my peace was gone. My King is also the Prince of Peace, so if my peace had left, I was not right.

Kingdom Key:
When your peace has left, you're not right.

About a week later, I was miserable inside. I had to go to one of my rental houses to try to fix the pool pump, since some glass got lodged in the screen. As I was trying to fix it, I cut my finger, and it started to bleed. That was it! I started praying and asking God to help me. I was trying to live for Him, but I was miserable and hurting. My wife was hostile. She was trying to move out, and didn't want our marriage to work. As I was driving home on Twentieth Avenue, a state trooper pulled me over. He asked for my license and registration. As he started to write me a ticket for speeding, I started to weep. This new King wanted to talk about the prayer that I had prayed a few minutes ago. The trooper looked at me, and asked if I was OK. The more he wrote, the more I cried. I was really crying hard and couldn't stop. The trooper asked again, "Mr. Coker, are you OK? What's the problem? It's only a speeding ticket." Because I felt this would stop him from asking me any more questions, I blurted out, "I am a new Christian, and I thought things would be better if I gave my heart to Jesus. I am miserable! Just give me my ticket so I can go home." The trooper put his ticket book down in the front seat and said, "Mr. Coker, I know this Jesus you gave your heart to pretty well." For the next forty-five minutes, sitting beside the road, that State Trooper prayed for the situation with my family and blessed me.

Continuing on he spoke gently, "Mr. Coker, since you're a new Christian, we have this course at my Baptist church called 'Survival Kit.' Would you like to come and learn how to survive?" God set me up! What else could I say but, "Yes, I sure do. I don't need to pray about this one any longer." I figured with all that prayer I was off the hook, but no, he still gave me a $158.00 ticket. "Obedience is better than sacrifice."

So, I went to meet the pastor, Randy,* at this Baptist church. I had a few issues to overcome about the Baptists and what I had been taught over my lifetime. At our meeting, he was very gracious. As I started to tell him my prejudiced beliefs about the Baptists, I exposed my ungodly judgments. As he spoke, the King living inside of me helped me to understand that there are *church doctrines* and there are **Kingdom principles**. They are not the same. This fresh reality hit me like a ton of bricks! Pastor Randy reviewed my dislikes and started addressing them one by one:

"So you think we don't believe in speaking in tongues?" he began. "Let's look at Acts 2," he continued. He showed me in Scripture and explained it. His answer surprised me. He said that he believed tongues is a gift from God, but it has been misused. He went on to tell me that if I had the gift, he was all right with it.

I said, "What about divine healing?" He wondered aloud if I was sick. I said, "No, I wasn't." "Then what's the problem? We do believe in divine healing," he said, as he read me the Scripture where the elders are to be called and anoint the sick with oil.

"What other questions can I help you with?" he asked. I complained, "Don't Baptists believe once saved, always saved?" The pastor asked me if I was saved. I said, "Yes, of course." Then he asked, "Are you going to stay saved?" I said, "Of course." "Then what's the problem?" he kindly asked. He hugged me and welcomed me to the family. I started "Survival Kit" the following Thursday night.

During this course, the Lord began to speak to me about corporate authority. He let me know firmly that if I exercised my gifts, and offended the authority to which I was submitted, that I would surely be in rebellion and would suffer the consequences. He showed me how to release the Kingdom without speaking in Pentecostal language. I learned to heal in Jesus' name without screaming. I even learned to give prophecy in parables. I studied and became an instructor for several Bible study courses including: "Survival Kit," "Experiencing God," "Search for Significance," and "Prayer Time." I learned so much from this fellowship.

There was a deacon whose sons weren't going to church. I used to hunt and fish with them. He asked me to do what my dad did with Tim. He asked me to witness to them. He was concerned and wanted them to return to church. I finally made him aware that the boys knew all the sin, gossip, and backbiting that the pastors and leaders were involved in. Therefore, they weren't interested in his Jesus. I told him I was powerless to be a witness. Even in my immaturity, the Father allowed Kingdom truth to be spoken through me. Philippians 4:8-9 says,

> *Finally, brethren, whatsoever things are true, whatsoever things are honest, whatsoever things are just, whatsoever things are pure, whatsoever things are lovely, whatsoever things are of good report; if there be any virtue, and if there be any praise, think on these things. Those*

things, which ye have both learned, and received, and heard, and seen in me, do: and the God of peace shall be with you. (KJV)

When God showed me in Houston that Pastor Randy was one of those many church leaders whose heart He had hardened and would not allow to spiritually father me, I felt sorry. But now I know why. Pastor Randy had a moral failure which destroyed many lives. This was heartbreaking to watch! I do know that he has since gotten some healing for himself and his family, and they are doing better now, but his sin affected the whole community. I do not regret the Lord leading me to that church. If I had not gone to this Baptist church, I would not have as solid a foundation in the Bible as I have now, nor would I have the heart to disciple people like I do.

Christmas of 1993 was a good, but hard time for me. Susie said that she was going to move back home for Christmas—only for the boys, but after Christmas she was out of there. One night in prayer the Lord quietly spoke to my heart, in a still small voice; but it thundered in my head. "She will not leave again. Stop walking in fear." Job 3:25 says, *"For the thing I greatly feared has come upon me, And what I dreaded has happened to me."* The Lord was trying to bring deliverance to me from the spirit of fear in my life. Job 3:25 also deals with the things you dread. When you give place to fear, you will have a spirit of dread. When Susie would tell me that she was going to leave, I would crumble in fear. After the Word of the Lord set me free, I was willing to serve God with or without her. So one day she got mad and told me that if I didn't do what she wanted, she was leaving. I boldly told her that I was the spiritual authority in our house. "If you have a problem with that, don't let the door hit you where the good Lord split you," I said. I took hold of the reins of authority in my home and the fear of her leaving was broken that day. I have seen fear of a spouse leaving steal the true destiny of many who have high callings on their lives. I thank God, He did not allow it to happen to me!

On February 14, 1994, Valentine's Day, we went to the church my mother and dad had attended for 45 years. Susie and I looked, and there were 20 couples at the altar renewing their marriage vows. It was just like the vision. Susie said she only did it to get me off her back, but we renewed our marriage vows that day with the others. From that day forward, we haven't used the word divorce once! (We have used murder, but not divorce.)

My business partner was also someone whom I feared. He was starting to become very displeased with my relationship with my newfound King, because I started to bring some changes to the company. Jesus started dealing with me about some of the business practices we were engaged in, like taking cash, and not reporting it. I really didn't want to deal with him on this matter, because I had started to make so many changes, and this was sacred cash.

After I argued with God for several weeks, He finally asked me if I was willing to confront the issue. He reminded me of the scripture in Job 3:25. I had given fear time to turn to dread. I finally told the Lord I was willing to confront my partner on this issue of not reporting sales. Immediately, peace came back to me, and my King said, "Great, I will handle it for you since you have now become willing." The burden to confront the issue was released.

About two weeks later my business partner came running into the office. He was mad and scared. He started yelling, "Your blankety, blankety wife is going to ruin us. I ran into her at the 7-Eleven today, and she still is going to divorce you. She said all she wants out of this marriage is what's fair, and she knows about the cash we take." He started telling me that we have to stop doing that and run every dime properly through the books. It amazes me how God used a spirit of fear to His advantage. All I had to be was willing.

Kingdom Key:
Unbridled fear will turn to dread. Dread will develop into depression, and depression will kill your dreams and destiny.

A little later, my business partner informed me that there was not enough room in the company for me and Jesus. He was forcing me to choose—I had to get rid of Jesus if I wanted to stay, or both of us needed to get out. God started showing me it was time to make a choice.

About this time I started to have angelic encounters and was being shown my inheritance in the Kingdom, specifically in Vero Beach, Florida. God showed me the spiritual principalities of darkness over the region and city, and how to defeat them. The realm of the Spirit was coming alive to me like never before!

The Lord sent a business opportunity my way in Orange City, Florida. It was a lighting store that a former youth pastor, who lived in Vero, had started. I began praying about a move. One night the Lord presented me with two choices: His perfect will, or His permissive will, for my life. He said that He would bless either one.

The Lord showed me that if I chose to stay in Vero, He would remove my business partner and prosper me financially more than I had ever dreamed. But if I stayed in Vero, He could not promise me that my family would stay together and be restored. I also knew God wanted to use me in ministry.

I knew it was a no-brainer for most, but Susie was still hurting, angry, and didn't want to be married. My kids weren't real happy about life with a father who had changed so drastically, either. The choice came down to money or family, which would I chose? I told God, "I am all in. Let Your perfect will be done in my life." The King, living on the inside of me, let me know He had a plan that was not only sufficient, but satisfying, if only I would follow Him. He promised me a ministry that would take me around the world! Susie and I came into agreement, and we moved to Deltona, Florida.

As I look back, I am grateful that the Holy Spirit trained me so fast. What I was about to walk into would have killed me, if I had not listened and learned about the Kingdom. I remember when the Holy Spirit spoke to me one night and said, "Charlie, I can do more in six months with a man who will obey, than I can with other men in sixty years. How badly do you want to mature?" I said, "Give me the fast track. I can handle it." So the Lord told me to cross out a scripture and rewrite it. He showed me 1 Samuel 15:22 and had me cross out, *"to obey is better than sacrifice"* and change it to read, *"Charlie, obey or you will become the sacrifice."* That's the fast track kingdom training course!

Kingdom Keys

1. The Kingdom incorporates everyone who has received the King. EVERYONE! Therefore, preferences are allowed, but not prejudices.

2. The Kingdom has a language of its own…True, Noble, Just, Pure, Lovely, Kind, and of Good Report…

3. Kingdom principle of business: Don't be unequally yoked.

4. Kingdom fast track training course: Obedience.

5. When your peace has left, you're not right.

6. Unbridled fear will turn into dread, dread will develop into depression, and depression will kill your dreams and destiny.

7. Every false accusation has enough truth that applies to your life, that you can use it to become more like the King. It requires a spirit of repentance and humility.

Round 4

Leave Your Father's House

Now the Lord had said to Abram: "Get out of your country, From your family And from your father's house, To a land that I will show you. (Genesis 12:1)

Personally, I love this passage of scripture. As you go on and read verse two, it states, *"I will make you a great nation I will bless you and make your name great and you shall be a blessing."* Verse three continues, *"I will bless those who bless you, and I will curse him who curses you; and in you all the families of the earth shall be blessed."*

This passage has taught me so much, because God told Abraham to leave his father's house and his family. This was a personal prophecy from God to Abraham. Pay attention to verse four, *"and Lot went with him."* It's interesting to note that because of Abraham's disobedience, he failed to have another personal prophecy directed to him until after Lot and Abraham separated. Genesis 13:11 reports, *"Then Lot chose for himself all the plain of Jordan, and Lot journeyed east. And they separated from each other."* The personal words from God about Abraham's destiny did not come till after Lot and he had separated.

Look at verses 14-18 in Genesis Chapter 12:

And the Lord said to Abram, after Lot had separated from him: "Lift your eyes now and look from the place where you are—northward, southward, eastward, and westward; for all the land, which you see I give to you and your descendants forever. And I will make your descendants as the dust of the earth; so that if a man could number the dust of the earth, then your descendants also could be numbered.

> *"Arise, walk in the land through its length and its width, for I give it to you."* Then Abram moved his tent, and went and dwelt by the terebinth trees of Mamre, which are in Hebron, and built an altar there to the Lord.

This passage of scripture has been instrumental for my understanding of God's calling, because I see that Abraham is a great man of faith in Scripture. As I study his life, I see the process, which God took him through, to make him that man of faith. From my viewpoint, Abraham acted like a *spiritual orphan*. Like me, he was always afraid to stand alone. I recognize this as a mindset of a spiritual orphan. It has taken me years to dismantle that way of thinking and feeling, and replace it with a proper understanding of Sonship.

Moving away from Vero Beach, where family roots ran back five generations, was very difficult to do. But the Lord showed me that it was vital in order for me to deal with some areas in my family, and that if I didn't relocate, He would not be able to heal us and make us a family.

We had made the decision to purchase the lighting store in Orange City. The first day in Deltona, after my father drove the moving truck back to Vero Beach, we loaded up in my Dodge SUV and went to get some pizza. As we drove out of the driveway of the small three bedroom, two bath house we had rented in a section of town that my family was not used to living in, my oldest son Jason said the most hurtful thing I had ever heard. He said, "Dad, look at the car we are driving. This thing has 120,000 miles on it, and it's the best vehicle we have. Did you see the house you moved us into? Dad, you're turning us into dirt balls."

Man, that statement hurt me to the core. The next morning, I went to the Lord about that statement and why it hurt so much. The Lord showed me that I had always given my family nice homes, in great neighborhoods, had been a good provider, but I had been their source and not Him. The Lord asked if I really wanted Him to answer the prayers I had been praying for my family. He showed me in a vision how He was going to strip me of my ability to provide for my family financially as I had before. He said, "When you allow Me to remove your ability to provide as in the past, and teach your family how to rely on God, then I will be able to cultivate Godly relationships with your family." He said that He would also take care of us as we learned about His faithfulness. It was so hard to have foreknowledge that the Lord was removing the grace I had walked in; grace that enabled me to make money, even as a backslidden Christian. This was the hardest season in business I ever had. For years, I had been able to make money in the lighting business, but I always had a partner who would help me. I was a natural salesman. Now, for the first time in business, I had to work on my weaknesses, which seemed to parallel my spiritual life.

Truth be known, I was a very poor businessman. I had great people skills, but I don't feel like I was a true entrepreneur. I strove harder and longer to overcompensate. I had always been a workaholic and was driven by fear of failure. I have come to the revelation that this is one of the main character traits of a spiritual orphan. I was beginning to realize that I truly desired to be in full-time ministry, and God was using my business as a training tool to show me how the Kingdom works and to mold me into His image.

Building relationships from scratch in a new town was very difficult. Away from family and friends, learning to walk with Jesus, and learning how to fit within a large megachurch was a little overwhelming, to say the least! Within a few weeks, the Lord spoke to me about becoming a member of Trinity Assembly of God Church, which had over 1500 members, and a private school for my boys to attend. The instruction from the Lord was very clear and precise: "I am sending you to a church to serve Me under a man who is My servant. But if you get your eyes off of Me, the snakes in this place will bite you and take you out! This is your test to pass or fail!"

It was a very basic clear instruction with a test at the end. As I looked at this, I saw that God was sending me to a church and not a man. He was God's servant, but there was never a promise to be mentored or fathered. "Lord what are you doing to me? I have this Kingdom view of the King and His Kingdom, and You are sending me into an old wine skin," I asked. I want to be very careful not to be disrespectful or be dishonoring to the Lord or to His servant, but this was the biggest test and training for Kingdom living I had taken. You may ask why everything I learn has to be a Kingdom view. If the Kingdom is anything, then it is everything.

The first Sunday that my wife and family went to Trinity, I walked down the aisle and shook Pastor's hand.* I told him that the Lord was sending us to serve him at the church, and asked if we could have an appointment or do lunch some time. Shockingly, he stated that he was too busy and that would probably never happen. As I was shaking his hand, I went into a vision and the Lord showed me those snakes He told me about. I began a three-day prayer meeting to make sure I had heard God, and tried to renegotiate my position of obedience.

The Lord started to teach me about authority and honor at a Kingdom level, in ways I had never experienced before. The Lord showed me Psalm 105:15: *"Do not touch My anointed ones, And do My prophets no harm."* The Lord spoke this to me within a couple of days. "You can't have what you don't honor." The Lord was telling me that I was learning to do war with honor and the principles don't change, even when the realm of authority does.

When God has shown you the snake side of a ministry, and then tells you to never speak evil about a pastor, and to protect him from his enemies, you learn that Kingdom culture always looks for God, and the goodness of God, in every relationship and situation. "People see what they are looking for." God was teaching me to look to Him in all things.

That pastor was, and still is, the best preacher that I have ever been in ministry with, by far. He would preach with wisdom and power, and people would get saved every Sunday. There I would sit in amazement at what God showed me, and then see the mantle of ministry cover him like a blanket, and the power of God would manifest. Soon, I learned that God had his hand on his life—you don't start with 27 people and grow to a 1500 to 2000 member church without God's calling on your life.

He was a professional CEO preacher and carried a spirit of excellence to a level I had never experienced before. He was a strong leader who left no room for misbehaving.

I learned about positional authority by watching how the mantle of ministry on my pastor worked as he stood in his office and preached. Notice in John 11:51: *"Now this he did not say on his own authority; but being high priest that year he prophesied that Jesus would die for the nation."* After study of this particular Scripture, I came to understand that there is authority and anointing due to the position. I call this *positional authority*. What I've come to realize is that many of the people in church look for positional authority and avoid the protocol of the Kingdom, which is only attained by pursuing a relationship with the Holy Spirit.

Not long after joining this church, I was getting restless, eager to do some teaching or preaching. One of the associate pastors told me that no one taught at Trinity until they had proven to be faithful for at least two years, with no problems. That rule ticked me off, and I was offended by this guy. Very abruptly I told him that God didn't send me there to sit on some stinking pew and rot. I told him that I would do what God sent me there to do. I had been teaching "Survival Kit" to new believers in Vero Beach before I came to Deltona. When I asked how I could use the training I had, I was advised that it was a Baptist course, and basically to sit down and do what I was told. At this point, I was beginning to become labeled as a man in rebellion. The day the associate pastor called me a wild stallion, I looked at him and said, "At least I still have the equipment to reproduce and am not a gelding like you." Believe it or not, I am working on another book called: "How to Win Friends."

I started telling God He had better do something, or I was going to have a hissy fit. Look, the Bible tells us to come to God like a child. Once in a great while, a hissy fit would work with my dad, but only if the reason was a noble one. If it were manipulating or doing stupid stuff, he would not tolerate it, whatsoever. People often tell me that I talk to God with disrespect, and they would be afraid to act that way. The difference is, I know when He is on His throne ruling as God, and when we are in the garden and He is Father. When He is in the garden, I can tell Him how I feel about where He has me, and how some of His other children are frustrating me and exposing some anger or fear where I need some help. Papa God has always been concerned about me and sometimes that's what it takes to move His hand in my favor.

I remember Papa God taking me to the woodshed and punishing me one day, and as I was crying, I sat down by the lake. He came and sat next to me and started telling me how much of a pleasure it was disciplining me. I said, "PLEASURE?! You have to be kidding me. You thought that was fun?" God said, "I didn't say fun! I said pleasure." "Explain please," I responded. He said, "It's not very often that I get the pleasure of disciplining one of My sons because he's trying too hard to please Me." Continuing further He counseled, "This is the kind of disciplining that will train a teachable son to rule the Kingdom in righteousness." So there are times you have to find Papa God in the garden and throw a hissy fit. A hissy fit with wrong motives will get you into a lot of trouble, so your motives have to be pure.

The revelation that I was receiving about the Kingdom was starting to take root deep in my heart. All the while I was witnessing a ministry at extreme levels of anointing and fruitfulness, I was having a revelation of a snake-character hidden in that church. One day while I was in church listening to this great preacher preach, I heard the Lord say, "I'm trying to bring you to a new level of maturity." I said, "Lord what does maturity look like?" He said, "Maturity is being able to discern the truth even when it's spoken from a liar." I watched, listened, and learned, and found that the gifts and calling of God are without repentance. Also during this season of our life, my wife and I were learning to communicate better and attempting to raise our children in a Kingdom culture.

The results of my hissy fit before God were this: I had gone with our music minister one Saturday night to Tampa. As we drove, I shared my testimony of how God had visited me personally, and how He had started healing my marriage. I shared how I had been taken advantage of financially, by an old business partner. The next morning at church, a guest speaker got up to speak the message. He started releasing a vision he had the night before. Here I am, sitting in the back of a very large church, and this man is starting to prophesy about a businessman who had been taken advantage of financially. God sent him to this church to teach Bible courses to new believers. He started prophesying about my life. I wanted to escape by hiding under the pew, but the music minister looked right at me, and said, "Charlie, he is talking about you." He publicly called me out, "Sir, come here, I need to lay my hands on you." He prophesied my life story. The preacher prophesied how I had been sent to that city, and to that church, to raise up new believers. As he laid hands on me, I was slain in the Spirit, and I landed at the feet of the pastor. After I got up off the floor and sat down, I spoke to the Holy Spirit, "There is nothing he prophesied that You have not already told me personally." Then the Lord said, "That word was not for you, it was for the pastor." The following day, the pastor called me into his office. He said that obviously I had clout with God, and he released me to teach "Survival Kit" to new believers.

When I started the new believer's class called "Survival Kit," they felt it was not going to be successful because it was a Baptist course. The Lord proved Himself faithful, and the classes doubled every term.

The lessons I learned at this church were more about segregation vs. congregation, or church vs. Kingdom. When leadership segregates, they can control and keep hidden areas in their lives. Leadership becomes hierarchal and less relational. Many of the leaders with whom I am in ministry today, have come from that ministry, and have found God to be faithful. I discovered later, from one of the board members of that church, who is a private investigator by trade, that he investigated me to try to dig up some dirt. I asked what his report to the pastor was. His report was that I was an open book, and brutally honest; there was nothing that was hidden in any way. One of the Kingdom principles God taught me a long time ago was, "If you can't talk about your past, you're probably still connected to it, or it still has influence in your life."

Trinity had become our family. My wife and I sang in the choir, which was over 150 strong, and the power of God would show up every Sunday. I was teaching "Survival Kit" and had started a men's group. I was flourishing in ministry, and my spiritual gifting was starting to emerge with great accuracy. There was a group of newly married men working together with older men. God set us on fire spiritually and we were starting to become a force to be reckoned with in our community. Although this church family had become our life, in the back of my mind I could still see the things that God had shown me. We could sense that something was going on behind the scenes. Several of the founding members, who had been pillars of the church spiritually and financially, were starting to be ousted. There were starting to be public displays with open rebukes coming from board members and outside ministries during services. There was a local church that started picketing outside the building with signs, trying to expose the sins of the church.

One night, I had this warning-dream for one of the men who served on the board. I visited his home and spoke to him, along with his wife, with a warning from the Lord, *"Touch not mine anointed and do my prophets no harm."* It's hard to tell a businessman to be careful how he approaches a leader. Even when you're right, there should be proper protocol, based on respect and rank. Senior leaders are ultimately responsible to God and then to the leadership around them. There are definitely defined lines of authority; many times it's only by discernment of the spirit that we can know where one line of authority starts and the other ends. There may come a point when leadership will not listen to the Holy Spirit or anyone else who has been put in a position to hold them accountable. That's when you have to completely trust God.

On October 16, 1996, a very clear and prophetic dream showed me that it was time to leave Trinity, and that's when we left. I was accused of being in rebellion, and that I would not submit to authority. The dream also gave me the indication that there was going to be judgment released against the church. Not only was judgment coming against the Church for wrath, but for mercy. When God judges with mercy, its purpose is always to draw us back to Him.

The following day, I was at a Promise Keeper's meeting in Jacksonville, Florida with 30,000 to 40,000 men praising God. I looked over my right shoulder and I saw the Glory Cloud of God coming over the top of the stadium. As I watched, the cloud began to settle upon me, and God started speaking to me spirit to Spirit; His Holiness was so intense I felt like I was breathing liquid love. I thought it was going to kill me. Embraced fully in the Father's love, the Lord started showing me how He wanted me to leave Trinity for a short season. I was to go to a smaller church, where the minister would receive me, and he would give me time to preach in his pulpit. In this particular encounter, the Lord showed me my calling, and how He was going to use me to awaken America in areas of racism and religious tradition. As the glory descended upon me, there was a 50-yard radius of everyone around me laid out under the power of God. He spoke, and I started debating with Him about my oldest son, who at the time was still wrestling with drugs, and about how my marriage was hardly bearable. The Lord was telling me to preach the gospel. I started quoting scriptures back to God: 1 Timothy 3:5: *"...for if a man does not know how to rule his own house, how will he take care of the church of God?"* My son, Jason, was battling drugs and there's no way I could have stood in the pulpit and preached the truth. At that moment, the Lord told me to preach in faith what He had promised me about my family. He said, "I will heal your son, and I will finish healing your marriage as you preach My word." As I was in the cloud of glory, God continued, "I am putting a mantle of My glory on you to do the work of the ministry. Charlie, continue to pursue the anointing (in you) for relationship and direction, so that the anointing that is (on you) will do the work of the ministry."

On the trip home from this Promise Keeper's meeting, I laid my head on the passenger side door and wept most of the way home. I pleaded with the Lord to tell me what He meant by "the anointing in me giving direction, so that the anointing on me would do the work." The Lord spoke instead, "I will bless whom you tell Me to bless." As I was talking to the Holy Spirit, I said, "Holy Spirit, bless Steve." Suddenly, Steve, who was driving was almost wiped out in the Spirit and started yelling! "Stop that!" I said, "What? I didn't do anything." Then, I said, "Holy Spirit, bless the guys in the back seat." Whoosh, the Holy Spirit manifested in great power, and they were laid out in the backseat of the car.

The following week, I had an appointment with the pastor, and told him that I was leaving. Sure enough, just like the dream, I was labeled rebellious and unwilling to submit to authority. It's amazing how God can show you something and let you know it's coming, but once it comes, you still have to choose to operate in the flesh or walk in the Spirit.

I marvel how Christians can so easily get caught up in gossip and slander, just like the dream had warned me. I was going to be labeled rebellious and unwilling to submit to authority. I was called a wild stallion. All the while I started preaching and using my gifts to expand the Kingdom.

Several months later, a local news station videotaped my old pastor at a topless bar dipping dollars. This particular scandal was shocking, to say the least. It brought division among family members, among church members, to a city and region, and the devil had a heyday. At first the pastor denied it. He claimed it was someone else. It was fascinating to see the things I learned as I watched how a large denomination handled situations like this. Needless to say, this local expression of the body of Christ was coming apart. My wife and I were still amazed, even after I had the prophetic insights that I had, which we doubted at first. How does a man with this much anointing, with this much power from God get videotaped in that situation? (But for the grace of God, there go I.)

As the exposure of corruption became obvious, the skeletons that people had kept locked in their closets started coming out in all kinds of accusations. There was talk about sexual abuse many years before. Some said that he was a drug dealer; others rumored that he took all of the board members to the topless bars in Orlando. Some of the rumors claimed to be backed up, and many were being played on national television. The district officials were very slow in their response. That alone left room for the enemy to destroy many people's lives, and their ability to trust in the Lord Jesus or His Church. But the Lord was always telling me to *"touch not his anointed and do his prophets no harm."*

The rumor mill gushed like a raging river; more skeletons, and more accusations were sent swirling through the news media, both local and national. All the while, the body of Christ was searching for the truth, in many cases unwilling to face the truth that this could actually be happening.

Several months before we left the church, my wife and I had a meeting with the pastor about my calling into the ministry. I struggled with business since I wanted to be in the ministry. Pastor tried to convince me that I should definitely stay in business and not the ministry. We had a discussion in which I told him I wanted to preach in his pulpit, and in no uncertain terms, he told me it would never happen. The problem was, the Lord had showed me that I was going to speak in that pulpit, but the pastor replied, "over his dead body." Without hesitation I boldly said, " You know, I believe God can arrange that."

The first part of the year after the scandal had been exposed, I had a prophetic encounter that gave me a message from the book of Esther. The message described where the Jews had a legal right to destroy all of their enemies, but God told them not to. That night I called the leader who was in charge of the church at the time and explained the word the Lord had given me. He released me to minister. So, the pulpit that the pastor said I would never preach in was now available for me to release the word of the Lord.

That night I preached, prophesied and made some bold statements about how God would use a Hittite or Jebusite to bring judgment upon His children. They would bring forth spiritual judgment and correction. I told the church that God would bring in a Hittite or Jebusite to execute a judgment of mercy. Biblically, we are supposed to judge ourselves lest we be judged, but in this situation the Lord said release, and He would bring in a non-Israelite.

I was told by one of the board members later that night that they were making a decision on whether to press criminal charges. They decided to obey the word of the Lord. They brought proper correction to the best of their ability, blessed the people, and released the rest to the Lord

Two weeks later, because the videotape had been released publicly by the news organizations, the State of Florida filed charges and charged the pastor with drug trafficking, kidnapping, and pistol whipping a man over drugs. The accusations were atrocious. All I knew was that he had plea-bargained for a lesser sentence.

Several months later the Lord gave me a prophetic dream. When I woke up, I read the story of how Sampson had lost his strength by the cutting of his hair. As I read the story I realized that when his hair had been restored, the Lord used him one more time. He pulled down the two pillars that held up the coliseum. At the end of Samson's life, after his hair had grown back, he killed more of the enemy in his final move than he had previously in his entire ministry.

As I read this story the Lord spoke to me about my pastor. He said, "When his hair grows back, the end of his ministry will be greater than the beginning." Of course, the Lord asked me if I would be willing to restore him back to the pulpit. I replied to Him, "I don't even like this man." It was also evident that he didn't like me. But the Lord showed me how much I had learned to love, honor, and respect him because of the calling and the mantle that was on his life. I told the Lord, if that was what He wanted me to do, I would do it.

As my wife got up that next morning, I shared the encounter I'd had with God about the pastor. I told her that the Lord had said, "When his hair grows back, his ministry will be greater in the end than the beginning." That morning, I opened the newspaper to read while eating my breakfast. The first thing I saw was a picture of my pastor with his head shaved, because he had been sentenced to prison. At that moment I came to the conclusion that my choices had better be righteous in God's eyes. I started counteracting in prayer all the word curses from the church leaders in our community. I came into more resistance from Christian leaders than the world. I was certain that the enemy would have a field day with the pastor's life, and anyone who chose to stand beside him.

One test that the Lord always challenged me with, was to ask me if I was willing to restore someone that I did not agree with, did not like, and didn't trust. (The pastor didn't like me or trust me, either.) But God always has a plan. I knew that the calling for ministry was on my life. I told God that I had made the choice for His perfect will, and anything less would not be tolerated. I took a day off and spent it with God, seeking His wisdom to be sure that I would never become a public disgrace to the ministry or Him. I made a covenant with God, giving Him permission to kill me and take me off the face of the earth before I created a scandal that became a reproach to His name. Several people feel that I speak about God killing me too much, but it sure does curb one's appetite for sin.

Kingdom Keys:

1. Maturity is being able to discern the truth even when it's spoken from a liar.

2. If you can't talk about your past, you're probably still connected to it, or it still has influence in your life.

3. When your history disrupts your present, it will hinder your future. So make your history His story.

Church Authority

Round 5

Surviving the Snakes of Church and Not Becoming One Yourself

This is one of the hardest lessons I've ever had to learn. Because of my gifting and personality, I have a tendency to be extremely critical. However, the Holy Spirit has taught me that being critical is unacceptable for walking in Kingdom principles.

One day I was sitting in church listening to the preacher preach. I was being both critical and judgmental of his delivery style and his insight into Scripture. The Lord rebuked me sharply, "Are you ever going to mature, so I can put you in a position of authority and use you to properly judge My house, or are you always going to sit in the seat of the scornful?" God told me that He would never use me to bring revelation of judgment unless I was willing to walk the person through the healing process, with the intent of restoring them back to wholeness.

Kingdom Key:
God will never release you to pronounce judgment unless you're willing to walk with the person to bring healing and wholeness, if there is repentance.

This is one standard that will make you count the cost before you speak…

I knew that the Lord was quoting Psalms 1:1: *"Blessed is the man who walks not in the counsel of the ungodly nor stands in the path of sinners nor sits in the seat of the scornful."* The Lord took me in a vision and showed me the throne He had prepared for me to rule from; it was a very high back chair. As I sat on this throne, there was a plaque over my head that read Son, then it changed to Priest, and it changed again to King. I saw these three plaques above my head, and the Lord spoke to me about the positions of authority He was trying to give me. Rather than using the throne as a source of praise and encouragement, I was using my seat as a source of scorn—THAT'S a problem. A plaque that had "scornful" written on it rose above my head. The Lord reminded me that I have authority, and He was giving me a place of honor in which to sit. The Lord started to chastise me about my attitude, my criticisms, my false judgments, and how they were the reason that I had turned my place of authority into the seat of the scornful. My eyes started tearing up, and I began to weep. HOW could I stop being so critical and judgmental, since it had become second nature to me? I prayed for the Lord to help me so that I could sit in my seat of authority, judge in righteousness, and make a difference in the earthly realm. The Lord began explaining to me that He would teach me how to sit in a place of authority, and that I would no longer turn that place of authority into the seat of the scornful. I would learn to judge properly. As I pleaded with the Lord to please help me, He turned my seat upside down and started driving three long nails through the bottom of the seat. They were driven so that when He turned the throne right side up, there were three nails sticking about half of an inch up out of the seat of the throne. The Lord spoke to me sternly, "When you sit in the seat of authority and feel My nails in your behind, you will judge rightly." When we judge and criticize incorrectly, we are removed from the ability to stand in a great place of authority.

Zachariah 3:7 says it best: *"Thus says the Lord of hosts: 'If you will walk in My ways, And if you will keep My command, Then you shall also judge My house, And likewise have charge of My courts; I will give you places to walk among these who stand here."* Scripture is crystal clear. You must walk in His ways, obey Him, then you can judge. Only then can you move in the heavenly realms, which are the courts of heaven and walk among them—in the realms of the Kingdom!

During my time at Trinity, it became apparent that some of the upper leadership were having moral issues and personal crises in their Christian walk. I only know of a very few of that church's leadership who did not backslide or fall into worldly things. Temptation starts from the top and can affect every member of the congregation. It will expose your weaknesses or confirm your strengths.

Needless to say, Trinity was crumbling from the foundation it was built upon. God still had His hand on the church; the plans for Trinity and the calling of the city were going to be fulfilled. God's judgment was the beginning of His move in the area. 1 Peter 4:17 reveals God's pattern: *"For the time has come for judgment to begin at the house of God; and if it begins with us first, what will be the end of those who do not obey the gospel of God?"* The Lord's judgment always begins with His people. Fifteen years later, I'm still amazed at the number of leaders who are still bitter, wounded, and resentful about what happened at Trinity. We have a city full of twenty and thirty year old young adults who witnessed, as children and teenagers, the judgment of the Lord. They use it as an excuse not to go to or be part of any church. I am pleased to report Trinity is doing very well today, and has recovered to be the lighthouse of God's Grace to the city of Deltona and the region.

On Father's Day weekend of 2010, some twelve years later after the pastor was put in jail, I had the opportunity to restore him back to the pulpit ministry. His hair grew back, and he still is one of the best preachers I have ever heard. Surprisingly, some of the leadership of our city was still angry, resentful and did not want to participate in the restoration process. Even some of my closest friends and associates, who had heard for over twelve years that the Lord had given me this mandate to restore him, were starting to question in their hearts whether or not they could participate that weekend.

Romans 8:28 states:

"And we know that all things work together for good to those who love God, to those who are the called according to His purpose."

This scripture has to be my all time Kingdom reference Scripture. If I had not gone through this season of my life and learned what I had, I would not be where I am today. So many times, the Lord teaches by example not only what not to do, but what you're supposed to do, and how to do it. At this time in my walk, I was starting to see how authority in the church system flows from the pastoral office down. The pastor is at the top, everyone submits to him, and everyone follows his vision. If you get out of line or sideways with him, he is obligated to let you know who is boss, even if God is speaking to you.

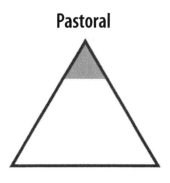

It started to become clear to me that the fivefold ministry was talked about, but never truly honored or engaged, in many congregations. In the church system, with a pastoral position on top, everyone submits only to the vision of that house. Protecting, covering, encouraging, and bringing people through their issues are all necessary portions that the church needs to continue to do. But, without the Kingdom focus it can become controlling, religious, and can miss the purpose to which God called that local church.

Please hear me clearly. I believe in authority structures. I believe in the authority of the pastor and the authority within the church. But with top-down only leadership it can become abusive and detrimental to your spiritual growth and development.

Kingdom Keys:

1. God will never release you to pronounce judgment unless you're willing to walk with the person to bring healing and wholeness, if there is repentance.

2. There is no greater sin than to commit the sin that was committed against you.

Round 6

The Word of Faith Church

"Behold the proud, His soul is not upright in him; But the just shall live by his faith." Habakuk 2:4

Just before leaving Trinity, I went to the Word of Faith Church in Orange City, the town next to where I lived. I met Pastor John,* a 6 foor 4, 255 pound, ex-con, who learned to box while in prison. He was, by far, one of the best Bible teachers I've ever sat under. He did line by line, precept upon precept, and knew the Word. I walked into his office that first time and said to him, "Pastor John, God has told me to come to your church." As I revealed to him that God had sent me, he opened his calendar and started picking the dates when he was going to let me preach. He said, "The Lord told me you were coming and needed pulpit time, so you could be trained for the ministry." God also told him the sins of another man had kept me out of the pulpit. God further related to him that I would be in his church for a season, and to give me as much pulpit time as he could. The faithfulness of God to open doors, where no man can, continues to blow my mind.

During the time that God used Pastor John to open doors for me to minister, I had an encounter with the Holy Spirit one weekend. I went back to Vero Beach to work on one of my rental properties. I was driving in my van, listening to a teaching tape on generational curses. In the middle of the teaching, the Lord spoke and said, "Do you believe generational CURSES are Biblical?" "Yes, Lord, scripturally, I can back that up." I replied. He continued, "Do you believe that generational BLESSINGS are Biblical also?" "Yes, I see that You are a generational God, all through Scripture," I answered. At that moment, the Lord asked if

I wanted the ministry mantle that my grandfather had walked in. My grandfather Coker died when my dad was 11 years old, so I had no personal knowledge of who he was, or what he was. The only details I knew about him came from the stories my father told me. Dad told me that one day my grandfather's boss had given him a WWI German trench knife for protection when he went to preach. My grandfather evidently preached a message of holiness that angered most of the religious people of his day. I don't know if he ever had to use the knife for protection or not, but the story always scared me. I asked the Lord, "If this prophetic mantle is a blessing from You, and if it's rightfully mine, can I have it?" The Lord told me my grandfather was a prophet to America, so I asked for his mantle.

Kingdom Key:
If you don't value your earthly inheritance, you won't redeem it completely for the next generation, nor will you discover your heavenly inheritance.

I did not realize that weekend was going to be an encounter with God about that mantle. I had a rental house, where I had the same tenant for over nine years. As I started to clean the house, I saw it was absolutely trashed. The renter had kept her dog in the garage, and it had urinated and pooped all over the floor. Trying to clean the mess up, I bleached the floor to get the smell out, but it wasn't working. I drove to the paint store, asked how to seal concrete to get rid of the horrible stink. The paint expert told me that I needed to use a two-part epoxy paint that came in three colors—gray, white and red. I was halfway through painting the floor when Holy Spirit invaded the garage. The Lord began to berate me about the stench in the house. He said, "The stench in this house is your fault! You've known for nine years that she had this dog, and you have a lease-contract that said no dogs were allowed. Since she paid her rent on time, you overlooked what was written in the contract." God clearly told me, "Don't start complaining about the stench in this house, when you were the one who allowed it to begin with." He went on, "You're just like many of My preachers. Just because someone pays their tithes and gives offerings, church leaders don't enforce My written contract. They overlook Scriptural principles because of their own comforts. If you're going to be my minister, you better keep to the written contract."

The Lord didn't stop there. He went on, "Look at the paint you're using, trying to seal the smell out. You had three choices of color, red, white, or gray. You didn't choose red, because red is too offensive. You didn't choose white, because white is too hard to keep clean, so you chose gray. That's just like many of my ministers, who don't preach on My blood, because it's too offensive, and fewer still preach on holiness because it's too hard to keep clean. They just gray it out, and then wonder where the power is. If you're going to be My voice, you'd better preach on my blood, and preach on a lifestyle of holiness through Me." At this point I was crying so hard, I had tears and snot flowing all over my paint job, all the while asking the Holy Spirit to teach me how to be His voice.

The Lord spoke and told me to go to Jack Hart's church on the north side of Vero Beach, up on the sand ridge. While I sat in the parking lot of this church asking God why I was sitting here, the secretary of the church pulled up asking who I was, and what I was doing. I told her that the Lord had been speaking to me about this church while I was praying. She invited me to go into the sanctuary and spend some time at the altar. She would let me know when she was leaving for the day.

After about thirty minutes of getting downloads from the Lord at the altar, the secretary told me she needed to leave and asked my name. I gave her my business card. As she pulled out of the parking lot, the Holy Spirit said to me, "Look over that fence." To my amazement, on the backside was a cemetery. I walked through the cemetery, and found my grandfather's grave. At the grave, I knelt down, cried out to God and begged Him to give me everything in my generational line that was a blessing. I also asked Him to show me everything in my generational line that was a curse, so I could confront it in order to be productive in the Kingdom.

I went into a vision, and was shown why my grandmother always prayed to see my father's last child. The day I was born, my grandmother was in the hospital with kidney failure. When she heard that I was born, they pushed her bed to the nursery ward. They held me up so my grandmother could bless me through the window. Then she charged my father to live a righteous life and raise me for the Lord's service. I believe my mother and father have obeyed her to the best of their ability. The following day she died. This event has always been a joke in our family—Dad says I was so ugly when I was born that I killed his mama. God also showed me that because of the fear of man, and the church system, my father was unwilling to walk in the mantle. So my grandmother carried it all those years, and handed it to me by the power of her blessing.

It's odd that my grandfather was a prophet, yet was also a member of the KKK. My grandfather's membership in this racist group was a clue to the root of the generational sins of prejudice and racism in my own life. It takes some willingness to do a little boxing, when necessary, to apply the curse-breaking power of the blood. My father became upset with me because of the sin I was exposing in our family. One day in the prison ministry where Dad was working, the Lord demonstrated to him that he had an ongoing problem with racism and needed to repent. I believe that the Lord told him, if he wasn't going to deal with his heart on this issue, that God would not be able to use him in ministry. I can tell you that in all the years since, he has been a blessing to African-Americans. He has had many of their pictures on his refrigerator, so he can pray for and brag about them. Some, who have come out of jail and prison, are doing ministry today. They tell me they are so grateful for my father in their lives. That's called redeeming your family line.

Pastor Jack Hart* called me a few days after spending time alone at the church's altar. The Lord spoke to him after his secretary had given him my card that afternoon. I didn't know at the time, but after my oldest son was born, Susie was attending Pastor Hart's Church. He had dedicated my son Jason to the Lord when he was just a baby. Pastor Hart completely opened up his heart and his church for me to minister. God was opening up doors that no man could open. Jack Hart had become the elder at the gate in Vero Beach for me, even though it is the place of my father's birth and mine. Personally, he was the apostolic doorway for me. I never ministered in Vero without letting him know where and when.

Kingdom Key:
It is vital to find the elder at the gates of the city who will bring protection to your ministry.

I was starting to operate in an extremely high level of the prophetic ministry, with no formal training, but with an extreme zeal for God. I was developing a reputation in our community as a prophet. Well, in the church system, that's not a good reputation to have, since there is very little room made for the gift. God develops the skill-set in us; but it is up to us to use it to expand the Kingdom.

God started waking me up at 4:44 a.m. every morning for weeks and weeks. When He woke me up, He would say, "You're my prophet. Don't be discouraged." Finally one morning I yelled, "What are you trying to tell me?" He said, "You finally asked? So look up John 4:44!" It reads, *"For Jesus Himself testified that a prophet has no honor in his own country."* The Lord told me this so that I would not let rejection control my love walk. So when I get depressed, He wakes me up at 4:44 and then I stop pouting.

During this season, we did ministry with a lot of people, but one couple who stood out were Mark and Phyllis Gregory. Phyllis was the best kids' minister in the county, and she was hungry for truth. God showed me her daughter sneaking out of her house at night and doing wrong stuff. Phyllis was offended, because she thought her family was perfect, and prophets were only to give words of edification. I was certain it was a clear, direct word for her family. She told Mark, and he confirmed to her that it was true. When she called to thank me, it started a relationship of trust, even though it was hard at times. Phyllis is a strong, gifted woman of God. She has a great calling, but she had some control issues that made us butt heads a lot. Every time Phyllis would come to a crossroads with God, He would tell her to call me.

I never offered her nice flowery words. It was always very blunt and to the point. For example, I would tell her, "You need to learn to submit to your husband!!! You're in rebellion in this area. Phyllis, I see you jumping on a spring board of impatience, into a pool of disobedience." I told her that a strong personality (another word for control) is something I understood quite well, since I was born into a family with three older sisters. I was the only boy, the baby, and my mother's favorite. (I was my mom's favorite because I was born on her birthday.) They tried to kill me most of the time. So, as a result of my upbringing, I don't baby women. Phyllis is one of the reasons God gave me that training. If you want to box like a man, get in the ring, and put on your big girl panties, and let's rumble!

Kingdom Key:
When you rumble in Love, you can live in peace in the Kingdom.

My time at the Word of Faith Church was critical, since the scandals at Trinity were capturing the people's attention in my city. National and local media were having a field day exposing all of the corruption within the church. The problem is, it's the innocent people who get hurt. Multitudes of them were running from God, because of what they saw and heard about the church.

Many a night I would walk and pray over our city, and ask God to heal it. All the while, God was teaching me how to operate in my gifting. He was teaching me to be gracious, loving, and kind, and at the same time bring revelatory information to leaders, who many times did not want to hear it. We began to host revival meetings with some of the traveling ministers who had flocked to Florida, because of the revival that broke out in Lakeland with Rodney Howard-Browne. The joy of the Lord was very needed in our region and churches. That anointing is still very important to my walk. Joy is one of the signs of the Kingdom—righteousness, peace, and joy in the Holy Ghost.

One night in prayer, the Lord gave me a revelation that Pastor John needed help battling a demonic spirit, which was being encouraged by his wife (a Jezebel-type). The Lord gave me very clear instructions. He told me to go to John, and let him know it was time to deal with the situation. The next day, I went by the church office to see him. I spoke plainly, "Pastor John, the Lord has given me a word for you." I started to give the revelation to John, but he did not receive it. This 6-foot-4, 255-pound man got physical with me, picked me up, and basically tossed me out of his office. I was completely shocked with what had just gone down. To clear my head, I went for a ride in the woods to be alone with God. I cried out to the Lord, "Why did it happen this way? Why did You let this happen to me? I thought You sent me! I thought he would receive me! I thought this was going to be a coming together and healing would happen." After 20 minutes of another major hissy fit, God gave me an additional word. He told me to go back to see Pastor John again the next morning. I was to tell him that while I was not the first prophet He had sent to him with this word, I was the last. If he did not deal with the situation in forty days, God was going to close the doors to his church.

The next morning I went as the Lord instructed me, and I sat with Pastor John. I said, "John, after the events of yesterday, I got alone with God to find out if I had missed it; if I had, I was going to come here and repent." I calmly told him what the Lord had spoken to me the previous day, emphasizing the forty day time limit that the Lord gave for him to change what was wrong. The answer he gave shocked me, "No, you're not the first, but we'll see if you're the last." Forty days later, the landlord decided not to renew the lease, and the church shut its doors.

One of the last times I ministered at that church, I was operating at a very high level with words of knowledge; the Spirit was giving me very precise details of people's lives. After I arrived home from the meeting, I tried to rest. The Lord wanted to debrief me about what went on during ministry time. As God clarified some things that I should have said or not said, He asked if I knew how the gift worked. I told Him I was getting used to it, and I was starting to feel confident. The Lord said that He was pleased with my love for the gift, but it was His and not mine. Then He told me He was going to take it from me for a season. I asked why, and He said that I didn't have the character to sustain a gift of that caliber. It seemed like the light bulb was turned off. I can tell you that from that day on, I was not very confident with personal prophecy. When I am on an assignment, I will get what I need from the Lord to do what He tells me to do. I still see regional and corporate stuff, but to this day, I operate at about 15% of what I did when He was training me. Personal prophecy is still the weakest part of my prophetic gifting.

I remember about six weeks after the gift was turned off, I walked up to three ladies who were standing and talking. I gave them a look and made a moaning sound, trying to make them think God had shown me stuff. With that, one lady started repenting for things that she thought I knew. When I got home, the Lord threatened to kill me if I ever did that again. It was then that I got mad, and told Him that this gift had given me a reputation. It was hard not living up to my reputation. Sternly He spoke, "I will give the gift back to you, if your church reputation is more important than Kingdom integrity. Or, you can be like My Son and have no reputation." At that point, I became the chief spokesman for the Kingdom.

Kingdom Key:
You can lose your reputation and still maintain your integrity in the Kingdom.

Almost 2 years later, Pastor John came to my store and asked me to support him financially in a Bible school that he was starting. I asked one question, "John, have you dealt with the situation that the Lord revealed to you?" He said, "No. I've been afraid to deal with that situation, because I don't want to lose my wife." The Lord showed me this verse:

> *For I have told him (Eli) that I will judge his house forever for the iniquity <u>which he knows</u>, because his sons made themselves vile, and he did not restrain them. 1 Samuel 3:13*

It's amazing how the fear of man forces tremendously gifted ministers to abort their true destinies and callings. I'm sad to say that a year later, Pastor John committed suicide. He was extremely instrumental in my growth on my own personal journey, and for that I am grateful.

I felt a stirring in my spirit; I felt like God was going to do something new. My paradigm was shifting from just viewing the Kingdom in the spiritual realm, to wanting to walk more in the fullness of it in the natural. I was starting to resent the systems of the church that I felt were bringing death and destruction to her people. If God had let me, I would've completely escaped the church system, but it was not in God's plan at that time.

As I was studying in 1 Samuel about Eli the priest, the Lord spoke to me, "You're going to make a move. I will no longer send you to a church; I will send you to a man." I said to myself, "Hallelujah, hallelujah!! Finally I am free!" I thought this would be an amazing change. If God sent me to a man instead of a church system, the man would undoubtedly receive me. He might become a spiritual father to me, or a mentor, perhaps even help me in my calling, instead of trying to prostitute my gift within his church system.

Remember Romans 8:28 says God works all things out. It is amazing how many people I was in ministry with then, that I'm now still doing ministry with today. My friend Greg, who was the children's pastor at Trinity, called me one day and said, "Hey, I have been promoted to associate pastor. You have to come and meet our new pastor." The meeting was set up, and I went hoping that he had a heart to restore all the damage had been done to the Church in the city. What a monumental task that would be!

On the morning that we met, the Lord spoke to me, "Remember, I told you I was sending you to a man, not to a church." As I walked in the door and met the new pastor of Trinity, the Lord spoke again and said, "This is the man. He is My priest, submit to him, come alongside him, and help him heal this church and the city."

At this point, Susie and I had been traveling as itinerant ministers for over a year. We slowed those plans, and very quickly we found our place to serve, and rebuild relationships. The Lord had definitely sent this man and gifted him with the skill-set needed to get the job done. God had given him a vision that he was to be a Joshua. He would cross over the

Jordan and bring this church into the Promised Land. Here I was, back at Trinity, helping to rebuild it from the foundation up. I was doing my part: traveling, running my business, and trying to keep a household intact.

Kingdom Keys:

1. If you don't value your earthly inheritance, you won't redeem it completely for the next generation, nor will you discover your heavenly inheritance.

2. When you rumble in Love, you can live in Peace in the Kingdom.

3. You can lose your reputation and still maintain your integrity in the Kingdom.

4. Find the elder at the gates of the city where you have been sent, who will bring protection to your ministry.

Round 7

Being Sent to a Man, not a Church

When I had the vision about God hardening the hearts of men of influence in my life, it was no surprise that Pastor Larry* was on the list. He was a man I loved, and for whom I was willing to lay down my life and ministry. I strove to please him, so that I could win his favor. If my father had been a full-time pastor of a church, he would've been a twin to Larry—same skill set and personality to boot. If I had known then what I know now, I might have handled the situation differently. However, I can never be certain since I was an orphan striving to be accepted, constantly striving to please Papa God. I was a lost child with a deep longing in my soul to be spiritually fathered. Problem was, Pastor Larry was also a spiritual orphan, just like my natural father. When two orphans are in the same house, there's usually trouble.

Trinity was beginning to turn around, but with so many people hurt, leadership had to be sensitive about the pace of the changes they sought to implement. Larry was a revivalist at heart and the church was Pentecostal. Best pay attention to the speed bumps ahead! Once the church started settling down from the crisis it had gone through, we got used to new leadership, their styles, functions and giftings. God was starting to show up again! One Sunday morning I was sitting in my second row pew in my fancy "leadership suit." The Holy Spirit asked me directly, "Are you a prophet?"

I said, "Lord, You said I am." He fired back, "I need a prophet on the wall today." He told me to go stand by a big tree that stood between the altar and the seats. Pastor Larry was midway through his message when the Lord told me to go stand by that tree. There I was standing by the wall next to this twenty-five foot tree, asking the Lord what He wanted me to do. The Holy Spirit continued, "You are a watchman on the wall. Watch this! I need you to watch what I'm about to do." All of a sudden, the wind of the Holy Spirit blew into the room. Pastor Larry stopped speaking; people came to the altar and got saved, healed, and delivered simply because of the presence of the Lord.

This started happening on such a regular basis that Pastor Greg and others were told to take their position on the opposite wall. It became obvious that God was going to move when we stood in our positions, so I asked the Lord what He was trying to accomplish.

The Lord said, "I am offering this church and its leadership an opportunity to function within the fivefold ministry. I'm asking you to birth the prophetic and to submit to the ones I send your way." Pastor Larry understood the fivefold ministry well, but he did have a problem with its function. It's one thing to have an understanding of something versus letting it function around you. The question was, could he allow it to function and flourish around him?

We started holding huge River Conferences and having some of the stars of the charismatic zoo come to the church. The speakers who came were extremely high caliber, and traveled on the revival circuit at the time. We were drawn into a season where we had extended meetings, and God was moving in a powerful way.

I was still traveling to New York to minister regularly. I would fly into Buffalo, rent a car, and then drive two hours south of Rochester to Hornell. I had been doing this for several years after the Lord showed me a vision about a coming move of His glory across this nation. He would send me to the triangular-shaped region there. When I would go there, the anointing was tangible. God had given me spiritual authority within that triangle of responsibility. God always showed me who the elders at the gates of each city were within the region. Many want authority but will not take responsibility. The Lord said if I would go once a month to New York, He would teach me how the Kingdom works in the heavenly realm, and then how it transfers to earthly arenas. So, once a month I would fly into Buffalo, drive through the little towns, repent for the sins of the churches and leadership there, and ask God for revival and healing. All the while God was teaching me about Kingdom functions, and how the apostolic works within those principles.

During one trip, God asked who I thought were the apostolic leaders of Hornell. We started talking about different leaders, and then He said that I would not be able to find them from the ground. So I rented an airplane to fly over Hornell. As the Lord showed me a church next to an old warehouse, He said to go find the church. He then gave me a word for the pastor. He had a word for her. I asked my sister, who lived in the area, if she knew about the church, but she didn't.

When I found the church, they were having an outing in the park down the road. I found the pastor, who introduced herself as Mother Brasswell. I gave her the word from the Lord about her being an apostolic leader in the city. She told me that for 26 years she had been pastor of this church in Hornell but she lived in Niagara Falls, a 2-hour drive away. She related how she'd watched all the big time ministries come and grow large, and then be taken out of the game by the enemy. She knew God had directed her to live somewhere else. I told her that the Lord would not let her live under the great oppression that was over this little city. The city is a spiritual switchgear. It was the same thing in the natural when the Erie Railroad maintenance shops were in Hornell. The blueprint seen on earth is the mirror of what is in heaven. This revelation has been vital for understanding how long to stay in a region and not be detected by the enemy. Mother Brasswell is still at her post as I write this book. She has to be over 90 and is still kicking the devil's butt.

God had shown me favor with some of the most influential leaders of that region. The Lord told me to go see Pastor Reid from the Tabernacle Church in Orchid Park, south of Buffalo. As the Lord opened doors for me to preach at that church, I saw it as a public sign of favor in the region. Pastor Reid is a true statesman in the kingdom. He would put me up in a house that the church owned on Prayer Mountain. He had me preach several times on Sunday nights. He was the one who had me preach the first service one Sunday morning. Tommy Tenney preached the second service following me. It was God's favor.

On another occasion I asked the Lord where the favor came from.

He reminded me that I had asked for the generational blessings from my grandfather on my dad's side, and I received his prophetic mantle. I thought that there might be some unused blessings on my mom's side, so I asked for any and all blessings that were legally mine from her side. Later I learned that the favor I was receiving came from the Albrecht family. Back in 1945 when this church was only a storefront in the city of Buffalo, the Albrecht family was in the Mennonite denomination. They had been filled with the Holy Ghost. Grandpa Albrecht had 13 children. Every year they would sell Christmas trees and ask God who the family should bless with the money as their family offering. I discovered this information when a lady at the church came to me after I preached and asked if I was Onalee Rigby's Son. I told her yes, and then watched as the pieces of the puzzle came together. See, my mother got saved at 13 and would go to the church camp up near Buffalo, where she met and was spiritually adopted as an Albrecht. My mother and several of the Albrecht girls were lifelong friends. When the Albrecht family moved to Florida, my mother wrote a letter to Aunt Ruth and told her that this was the last winter she was going to sleep in the cold; when she got to Florida, she was going to find a husband. In the summer of 1948, there was a tent meeting held in Vero Beach with a female evangelist. My father and some of his friends showed up, and the rest is history. From that revival, the First Assembly of God in Vero Beach was birthed.

The favor that came from asking for the generational blessing has blown my mind. My mother was not of an earthly line but of a spiritual line. You can get generational blessings from the spiritual relationship. This is how the Kingdom works.

On one of these ministry trips, I was going up a hill in a rented Ford Explorer. I pushed the car to its limit as the hill gradually steepened. When I topped the hill, the Holy Spirit spoke to me and said, "You wouldn't treat your vehicle that way, but because this is a rental, you have no problem abusing it." He started relating my abuse of this rental car to the grief that I was giving Pastor Larry. The Lord said that I was treating Larry like a "rent-a-pastor," and I had better straighten up and fly right. The Lord told me to start honoring him. I had a vision, and God showed me why I was so frustrated with Pastor Larry. In this vision, the Lord helped me understand that Larry's whole life had been preparation for this season. He had been prepared to function as an apostle and a spiritual father to the body of Christ. God showed me great details, and how the devil had exposed the sin of the church in the last season, even at a national level. If Pastor Larry functioned as an apostle in his leadership, God was going to release a billboard of His grace. This church would be a sign and a wonder, and it would represent the Kingdom and all of its Glory.

Just I was finishing this encounter with the Lord about my pastor and our church, my cell phone rang. It was Pastor Larry. He asked when I was coming home. They had extended the meetings another week, and said the Lord told him to have me preach on Monday night. I told him that I had just been given a word, and that I could be back in town late Monday afternoon, and would preach Monday night. That night, I prophesied with profound accuracy (his words) for 45 minutes. I publicly declared that he was an apostle. However, he had been unwilling to function as one, since his apostolic gift was not honored in the system into which he was birthed. Only his role as pastor was honored and recognized. I explained that Satan had made a spectacle out of the church at the national level, and God wanted to make this church a billboard of His grace for the world to see. The Lord said that Pastor Larry would have to take the church out of its denomination and become independent. He would be able to function in the fivefold ministry at the level he was called to. The Lord revealed that in 40 days a new movement would begin on Mother's Day.

That night I charged the leadership to judge the words I had given. Pastor Larry and the leadership of the church were in agreement. They made 350 tapes of the prophecy and handed them out the following Sunday. He also called a fast for the 40 days until the Mother's Day service.

Mother's Day came and Pastor Larry called nine different leaders who had been functioning in their ministries to the altar. For the first time as an apostle, he prophesied over us, laid hands on us, and commissioned us to fulfill the calling on our lives. It was profound for the Lord to pick Mother's Day. I believe the Brownsville revival, which impacted the world, was birthed on Father's Day. It served as a restoration of what was old. This fivefold ministry birth needed to be on Mother's Day, because it was a birthing of a new movement.

Over the next few months my traveling ministry started to take off. I was seeing great unity in the cities and churches where I was preaching, and the Lord was using me to bring churches and ministries together corporately. I was finally starting to see some fulfillment of the promises God had given me. Returning home from one of my trips, I was in a morning church service. As the pastor was preaching, a man that I didn't know was standing next to "my" tree. This guy looked like a sergeant-major in the Army. I asked the Lord who this person was. The Lord said to me, "He is a Senior Prophet, and I have sent him here because you have cried and whined about wanting a mentor. He is now your authority in the prophetic. Submit to him."

I went and introduced myself to Reggie Parker.* I told him who he was in the Kingdom, that God had told me to submit to him and that he was to be my mentor. There was a little problem…we had a major personality clash. For over a year, I felt as if all he ever did was give me instructions and a hard time. I felt he loved my friend, Pastor Greg, and that ticked me off a lot, because it seemed as though he did not like me.

One Thursday morning, Pastor Greg asked me to come and teach chapel at the school. Just before I began to speak, Reggie came to me and said he had a word from the Lord. He said God told him that I was arrogant, prideful, I had offended my pastor, and I needed to repent. As soon as I was done teaching chapel, I went to the pastor's office and said, "Pastor Larry, I'm arrogant, prideful, and if I have offended you, please forgive me." He said that to his knowledge he had not been offended, and he didn't believe any of those issues were true. As I left the office, Reggie was waiting in the hallway. He asked, "Did you repent the way I told you to?" I said, "Yes, but Pastor didn't know anything was wrong and said we were good. I repented anyway." Reggie started walking down the hall with an attitude, so I asked what his problem was. He let me know that he had told God that he would not mentor someone unless he would blindly obey him with no questions asked. I passed that test, but he only mentored me by demand. For the next few years we were like oil and water. He had a great gift, but was a horse's a_ to me. I honored his gift, because I wanted what he had. The problem with the relationship between us is that we were both gifted orphans.

Just a side note…a few years later, the Lord told me to call Reggie and tell him I had a word for his church. I told God, "Reggie can hear You; if You want me to preach in his church have him call me." That night, Reggie called, "The Lord told me that you're stubborn. You wouldn't call me and tell me you had a word to preach at my church." I consented to go to his church and give the word. Before I went, I sent out an email to the locals about my preaching on Thursday night at Reggie's. The crowd was so much larger than normal, his wife Gina said that I should be the pastor. LOL.

When Reggie stood up to introduce me he said, "I'll tell you what I like about Charlie Coker…" It was as if he froze in place, and the cat got his tongue. After 45 seconds, he started looking hard at his paper to find something good to say about me. At that point I yelled, "It's OK, Reggie. Everybody knows we respect each other, but we don't get along." He regained his composure, and told everyone that he admired me in spite of myself, because no matter what, I never stopped pursuing God. Ironically, I spoke on offenses! Now fifteen years later, Reggie Parker is part of the advisory board over my ministry.

Around this time, I began to sense that God was about to birth something new within me. He began with the River Conferences and extended meetings for revival. Could it be that the King who had walked through the wall, changed my heart and introduced Himself to me as a supernatural God, would begin to show me His Kingdom in a greater dimension? I began to feel that my days of usefulness at this church were coming to an end.

Charlie Coker, the businessman, had written large checks to support those conferences, which served to birth revival. The more checks I wrote, the more my pastor would say, "You can't outgive God." He urged me to give more, even though my company was struggling. "Give, keep on giving, and give by faith," he would tell me.

One Sunday morning, the checkbook looked dismal and the pressure to quit had come to a point of a showdown. Instead of going to church that morning, I went to my office and grabbed a phonebook and the Bible. I threw both of the books on the floor and told God one of these two books was going to give me an answer about the future for me and my family. "You can speak to me through Your Word, or I will find an attorney in this phonebook. I will file for bankruptcy and quit the business." The Lord spoke to me and told me to go to Psalms 107:27-28:

They reel to and fro, and stagger like a drunken man, And are at their wits' end. Then they cry out to the Lord in their trouble And He brings them out of their distresses.

Man, I was at my wits end! I pleaded with the Lord and asked Him to deliver me from my distress. He gave me a very clear word. "Charlie, you have stolen money from your vendors and have given the money to the priest, my pastor. You think it is blessed, because the priest said so. I consider that money stolen." He ordered me to go through my vendor invoice files, call out their names one by one, and repent for stealing their money. The Lord then told me not to sow finances out of the business until my company was paying its bills on time.

Susie and I started tithing and giving offerings only from the salaries we took home. A church father will continue to put demands on you, even when you're out of balance. Kingdom fathers get involved and make sure you're in balance.

Let me put a disclaimer on this: I believe in tithing and giving. I believe that there are times that God will ask you to sacrifice and give. In this case, you must hear the voice of God and not be manipulated by man.

Pastor Larry called me into his office about six months after I had given the prophecy about Mother's Day. He said the most unusual thing to me. I'll never forget it. He said, "Charlie, I believe that was the word of the Lord, and that is His perfect will. But if I take this church out of this denomination, we will lose too many people. I have chosen not to do it." After that I got up, shook his hand, and told him that I was going to obey God to the best of my ability, because I was promised that I would be a billboard of His grace. I thought it would be working beside him in ministry, but I was wrong.

I remember sharing the mandate with Pastor Larry about how God asked me to be instrumental in restoring the former pastor back to the pulpit when his hair grew back, but instead of helping me, he would start churning inside. I know how challenging it is to work at restoring someone if you were the one who had to clean up the mess left behind. At times I would ask, "Pastor, have you forgiven him?" and he would give a flippant answer. I would tell him, "Biblical forgiveness means coming with a verbal request; it isn't lip service. It requires a physical willingness to restore or repay. Are you sure you have forgiven him?" I asked. When I finally did restore the former pastor in 2010, Pastor Larry was my worst critic. He totally missed the Kingdom principle, but that's what orphans do.

I had a really bad situation with a pastor in New York who was an elder at the gates of Hornell. I had built a relationship with him for years, and we were good friends. I was well received by his congregation. We held multi-congregational meetings, were starting to network at a regional level, and I had come to speak in a three-day engagement in the area. All weekend we experienced the moving of God, but early Sunday morning, the Lord woke me up. He gave me a word that I knew was correction, direction, and even a warning. I gave a copy of the message to the pastor, and he approved it. As I spoke, I went into a vision, and was shown that the destiny of that church was hanging in the balance. I started to weep, tried to explain the severity of the message and even predicted that some leadership marriages would come to divorce, if things did not change. I declared that the church would have to close its doors, if they didn't respond to the Lord. The whole message focused on God's desire to change the language of the pastor, and for him to speak with kindness to others.

I had made a covenant relationship with this man. God had given me a very good understanding of the concept of covenant. I knew from my experiences that true covenant would always be personally costly. As an example, look at the covenant that God made with Abraham in Genesis 15:7-18. God took a bull, cut it in half, and walked between both halves. I know that when I am told to make a covenant, the "Cut the Bull" anointing will show up. I make covenant totally intent on God's perfect will. If those with whom I make a covenant are only interested in God's permissive will, a crisis always occurs in the relationship. As a result the covenant is usually severed. Sometimes it's time to "CUT THE BULL" and then hear God say His promises to us like He did Abram. The "ham" or name change, was not added until the test of the covenant was completed as in verse 18: *"On the same day the Lord made a covenant with Abraham."*

You would think that it wouldn't be a big deal, right? But two weeks later, when I was called to his house, two board members, his wife, and he had decided to persuade me to retract what I'd said. Being the orphan that I was, I decided to challenge them, since I felt bullied and pushed into a corner. As the discussion escalated even further, I called him an Ahab and her a Jezebel. My comments were not wrong—I was just not wise doing it in that situation. One thing led to another, and my own battling orphan spirit tried to defend my identity as a prophet. Had I been more mature, I would've agreed, repented, and walked away. But at that time I couldn't. A prophet named Jim, was on staff of the church. He decided to challenge me face-to-face. To make a long story short, most of the fruitful ministry I had been doing in New York came to a screeching halt. I got so mad that I wrote letters to the board members of the church. I let them know, in no uncertain terms, that I was willing to fly from Florida, meet them in the town square, let the God who answers by fire show up, and kill the one who was wrong. I reacted this way because my identity had become wrapped up in my gifting. This little escapade cost me relationships with some of the biggest churches in the region. Even though I felt justified, I should have asked the Lord for the right words, since mine weren't received well. As I drove back to the Buffalo airport, I was completely devastated and was asking God what happened. He reprimanded me because I had put this relationship above the covenant with Him. I had also put too much responsibility on man, and not on Him. I felt like I would never fulfill my calling, or see the promise of revival in New York.

Pastor Larry and Reggie made me cancel my traveling schedule for the rest of the year. I needed that time away to heal and learn some life lessons. As I cried about the New York region of ministry, God told me to let it die. If I would let it die, I would reap the increase in other regions. One of my prophet friends told this story in a book he wrote on what to never do in ministry. He said to never tell a woman to her face that she is a Jezebel and that her husband is an Ahab. She will murder you. Everything came crashing down, and I really didn't want to ever return to New York. Pastor Reid from Buffalo was preaching at one of the River Conferences and asked me where I had been. I assumed that he had heard what had happened between me and the pastor in Hornell. Pastor Reid took me aside and fathered me at a very critical time in ministry. He said he had heard what happened, had also heard that I had repented a few times. "I never thought you were a quitter," he said sadly. "The pastor is a hotheaded Italian from the Bronx, and he may never forgive you. I believe what God showed you about revival is from Him," he said. He prayed for me and asked me to let him know when I was coming back to New York.

Over the last 12 years, I've sat down seven different times and tried to repair this broken relationship. First, I went as a young immature prophet, then as a traveling evangelist, and finally as a maturing apostle. I got so tired of repenting; it started to make me sick until one day the Lord showed me Matthew 5:23-25:

> *Therefore if you bring your gift to the altar, and there remember that your brother has something against you, leave your gift there before the altar, and go your way. First be reconciled to your brother, and then come and offer your gift. Agree with your adversary quickly,*

while you are on the way with him, lest your adversary deliver you to the judge, the judge hand you over to the officer, and you be thrown into prison.

My wife Susie has a saying, "When you extend the olive branch of peace, make sure it still has leaves on it, or it's just a switch and brings more wounds." The Lord spoke to me about the fivefold ministry, which are gifts found in the book of Ephesians. Yet they are not greater than the relationship with a brother. If we would lay our ministry titles down, and reconcile with our brother first, maybe we could start manifesting the Kingdom and not be trapped in some hierarchal system that brings death rather than life. The last time I met with this pastor, I met as a brother, truly concerned about him as a brother, and not a minister. "They will know them for their Love, one for another." After that last meeting, God released me from trying to restore this relationship.

The sad thing to report is that the pastor and his wife are now divorced, and many in their church leadership are struggling with their walk with the Lord. The associate pastor, Jim, and I became very good friends, and after the situation, we walked together. I tried to help him for six years to forgive this pastor and the church system, to no avail. We were accountable to each other as we both pursued God, but Jim would not walk in love and allow God to heal him. He refused to let God remove the bitterness in his heart toward this pastor and the church.

Jim was a strong prophet. He would eventually come to a place in his journey when he needed to repent and forgive, but he guarded his bitterness. Each time he got a toe infection, it remained as an open wound until he repented. This happened at least six different times over several years. Jim eventually got divorced and moved a few hundred miles away. One day I was talking to him on the phone and asked a very simple question? "Jim, are you living with a woman?" Boy, did that send him over the edge! He wrote me a nasty email telling me I was as judgmental and critical as the old church system was, and he was done with our relationship. I asked the Lord how to respond. He told me to send him an email asking for forgiveness for offending him and invading his personal space. I also had to admit to him that I had not realized our relationship had changed. Since I could no longer hold him accountable in those areas, I needed his forgiveness. A few months later, Jim's toe infection came back, and he wound up in the hospital. I asked the Lord if I should fly to New York and lay hands on him to heal him. The Lord said, "No, he had his opportunity, and he chose not to walk in forgiveness." A week later, his toe infection spread to his bloodstream, then his heart, and he died. He was 50 years old.

This Kingdom principle of love is a must. The Lord gave me a quote to live by: **"Charlie, if you cannot love by your standards, you cannot live by them either."** This was a hard lesson for me to learn, because in the last season I had become very religious, and dogmatic in my belief system. Let me put it in Susie's words, "I had become a religious jackass."

Kingdom Key:
Love MUST be the standard for operating in the kingdom.

When it came time to leave Trinity, I made up my mind that before I left, Pastor Larry was going to give me his blessing, (which he never did.) I had been labeled rebellious and not submissive, but I had purposed in my heart that I was going to get his blessing one way or another. Needless to say, I overstayed my welcome. I told God that if He was going to make me leave without his blessing, then I wanted a prophet to call me out publicly, and tell me that I wasn't welcome at that church anymore.

One day, Kingsley Fletcher, a major prophet who had preached at the River Conferences, was leading some meetings at the church. He called me out. He chastised me publicly and said, "You aren't welcome here anymore. You aren't liked, and you are staying here because you covet the blessing of a man. You are in rebellion to God and need to leave." That got me in trouble big time both with Pastor and Dr. Fletcher. The pastor rebuked him, and I had to tell them both that I forced God's hand. Both of them were mad at me, but I finally got the word I needed. Because I was still dealing with a man-pleasing spirit, I still did not leave. I continued looking for blessing and approval before I moved on. About six months later I was hunting in Georgia. While sitting in a tree stand, complaining to the Lord about how my walk had become dry and difficult, the Lord spoke abruptly to me, "You can dry up and blow away, as far as I'm concerned. You had a man publicly sacrifice his ministry to dismiss you from Trinity, and you still won't leave. Don't complain to Me about being spiritually dry." I called home from the tree stand and told Susie, "We are looking for a different church next week."

It was sad to see that the nine leaders Pastor Larry released to do what God had told them to do had no relationship with him, or the church after a year. He had missed the great opportunity to father, but instead he craved power and control. All nine of us felt that the control and top-down system was not the kingdom. To this day, all of us are in ministry doing what he spoke over us. A few of us are still in ministry with each other.

Out of the nine ministries that were birthed that day, I was the only one who pursued relationship with Larry for years. I knew that the Lord had sent me to a man, not a church or a system. I was getting really frustrated as I waited. When one is an orphan, he will not have the capacity or understanding to serve as a spiritual father to others. I had a crisis, because I knew God had shown me what was supposed to be done, but it was out of my control. God had also told me that revelations and new teachings about the Kingdom that were given to me would be preached from the pulpit of Trinity. The only problem was I thought it was me who would do the preaching. One of my employees, Marsha, went to Trinity. She would hear about my fresh revelations at work. Then, I would go have lunch with Pastor Larry, and for the next three weeks, he would preach my messages from the pulpit. Man, that would make me mad! I told God one day that it wasn't fair! That's when He told me He was working on my EGO. (Edging, God, Out). "Are your messages getting preached at Trinity like I told you?" "Yes Lord, but I thought if You gave the revelation to me, I would be the one preaching them." I complained. "That's your problem; you thought and did not ask. My ways are higher than your ways, remember?" God firmly said.

My friends came to me saying that they heard God. God had told them that I had to go to a Morningstar Conference. I was in no mood, so I told them if they believed that it was God, they had to pay all my expenses to attend. They did! In the middle of the first night of the conference, I entered into a prophetic dream. In the dream, I was trying to convince Pastor Larry that I had a $10,000 builder's note, which looked like a stock certificate. I knew it belonged to him and was trying to get him to take possession of it. I had people waiting outside that room for me to get rid of this $10,000 builder's note. I debated and argued, but he would not take ownership of the note. I awoke from the dream, and the Lord spoke to me saying, "What you have is valuable, but you can't force even things of value on someone who does not want them." I went back to sleep and returned to the dream. I revisited him one more time, wound up arguing, and trying to get him to take responsibility and ownership of the note again. It had his name on it. I let him know, "You're an apostle, you're a builder, and this is a $10,000 builder's note," but he would not receive it.

In the dream, people connected to me were starting to get angry with me, since I would not move forward until this note was given to its rightful owner. Many of them told me to just keep it myself. Then all of a sudden, Pastor Greg came to me and said, "Listen, I've told everybody to give you time and space, because you will not take something that's not rightfully yours. Charlie, he's a pastor. Don't make him take ownership; give it to him as a gift." I answered, "That's a great idea! I will give it to him as a gift." I returned to the office; I humbly said to Pastor Larry, "I'm giving you this as a gift, free and clear no strings attached." I handed it to him, and he received it with gladness. He then walked over to the front of his computer, took the certificate and put it in the front of his computer. The computer sucked it inside, and a few seconds later spit it back out. It sucked it back in, then spit it back out. Pastor Larry took the certificate, handed it to me, and he made this statement. "My system can not take this." I came out of the dream, and the Lord spoke, "When are you going to stop trying to make people take ownership of the Kingdom system, when they won't put down their church system first? Stop trying to force people." He was planning to open doors, and I had to make a decision and not look back. God said, "No regrets. This is part of your journey."

> *Most assuredly, I say to you, unless a grain of wheat falls into the ground and dies, it remains alone; but if it dies, it produces much grain. John 12:24*

At that same conference, Rick Joiner introduced a guest speaker who had not been scheduled. Kingsley Fletcher! I was sitting in the middle of a large crowd, knowing that God had heard my cry. Dr. Fletcher called me out by name. He, Jack Deere, and several others spoke a word over me that released me from the old system. They gave me marching orders for the new system. The word explained why I never seemed to fit in the local church. I've seen this pastor-driven triangle system long enough to know that it does not work long with kingdom principles.

Kingdom Keys:

1. If you cannot love by your standards you cannot live by them either

2. Love is the standard for operating in the Kingdom.

3. When you extend the olive branch of peace, make sure it still has leaves on it, or it's just a switch and brings more wounds

Apostolic Authority

Round 8

What Do You Do When Your Reality Check Bounces?

The middle rounds of every good boxing match can be grueling to say the least. This was the most difficult season of my journey. I had been away from New York for more than two years and really didn't care about going back. Then the Lord started reminding me of the revival that He promised would come to the region, and I would get excited all over again. I began to push for God to do something supernatural. He caused me to remember that in order to regain regional authority, I had to walk back into the area that had murdered me. And... I had to do it in love. The devil can't ever handle love. Some of the people I had offended would not forgive me, but God would grant me greater authority, if I continued to take responsibility over the city and region. Authority is granted to the ones who take responsibility.

I came out of the last church experience extremely hurt, wounded, and to be honest with you, angry at the church system. If God had let me, I would have printed bumper stickers that read "Church Sucks" and put them on the car of every pastor I knew. But my King, who is inside of me, wouldn't allow that. Meanwhile, He was giving me revelation on how His Kingdom should function, but it just wasn't adding up in the natural.

I had been building a strong connection with Apostle Tim* in New York. I began to be exposed to the apostolic and how it functioned within the house church movement. I liked what I heard. I liked what I saw, and it had some of the Kingdom principles that I knew God was showing me. Apostle Tim and I continued our relationship when I traveled to New York. His ministry was one of Prophetic Deliverance. Boy, did Susie and I need some of that! His ministry brought more inner healing than anything we had been involved in before. Coming out of the church system, wounded, coupled with creating my own problems in New York, I was one big mess.

His team had set up a deliverance session in a hotel room in Buffalo, New York. Ironically, the day before our session, I ran into my aunt in Hornell. During our conversation, she started telling me that my maternal grandfather used to be in senior leadership at the Masonic Lodge. I had never known that! During the deliverance sessions in Buffalo, a team member had a vision of a demon swinging at me with a high-ranking Masonic Lodge ring on it's finger. It still amazes me how much garbage we deal with in our generational lines. Just remember the cross and the blood of Jesus cancel all curses. When the effects of those curses linger, we need to deal with them directly and properly.

I started believing with all my heart that the apostolic system would be the one to replace the church system. The problem with this belief system is that we are all of the same family, and because of our differences, we can be at odds with each other. Some of the people in this movement believe that the house church movement is God's new thing, and anything with a building is demonic. With all my hurts and wounds, I became like Saul before he became Paul. I was zealous over the new revelation and was running from anything that looked like the old church structure. I started catching the apostolic in the light of this triangle.

Apostolic

Now, therefore, you are no longer strangers and foreigners, but fellow citizens with the saints and members of the household of God, having been built on the foundation of the apostles and prophets, Jesus Christ Himself being the chief cornerstone, in whom the whole building, being fitted together, grows into a holy temple in the Lord, in whom you also are being built together for a dwelling place of God in the Spirit. Ephesians 2:19-22

I love this verse! It clearly states that WE ARE citizens of the Kingdom, the household of God, where the foundation is built upon the apostles and prophets, who are built on Jesus Christ, the chief cornerstone. The final line is key. This all takes place "in the Spirit."

Through my experiences in the apostolic house church movement, I have come to embrace the fact that God is absolutely flowing through the house church movement. I believe the revival, that God has mandated for this nation and the world, will not thrive or be successful without the house church movement blending with the Kingdom message. The key is the unity to blend both systems.

During this time with Apostle Tim, I had a wise elderly gentleman in Buffalo pull me aside one afternoon. He said, "Son, I know this apostle you're talking about. I want to give you a piece of advice and a warning. You're a businessman, and I have watched and observed him with other businessmen. When you can no longer pay and be a benefit to him, you will be discarded." I tucked this information in the back of my mind.

We started building a house church network in Florida, and used our relationships and influence to build a prophetic team to provide deliverance and sponsor mini conferences. We provided permanent housing for Tim and his wife, supported them when they traveled to conferences and deliverance sessions, while building the network.

The office of apostle is a foundational gift. When it is applied properly, the apostle elevates people from below, pushing others up into their gifts and callings. The office releases an individual to be all that God has called him to be. There's still an authority structure, but this position is at the lowest point pushing upward for the betterment of individuals. That all sounds good in theory, but there still has to be submission to authority.

Our small group had property in New York that was going to be a pastors' retreat where all the hurt and broken pastors from the old church system could come and be healed. I can remember Apostle Tim telling me that he would not be a spiritual father to me. We talked about it, and he said there was no way that he could do it. Again, I wondered why still another leader in my life would not father me. As I look back now, I can tell you. He was a spiritual orphan himself; he had his own father issues, which he had carried for many years. His father is in the ministry, and he had some of the same hurts, wounds and complaints that I did. Tim believed his calling was to grab as many people as he could and help them escape the church system. We had no problem with going into the church system and blowing it up, because it was for the greater good. He believed that God was done with the church system. This is not what I believe now. I believe I am called to help the church turn to the Kingdom and become the glorious bride.

This season of my life was some of the best training I ever had. We performed over 130 deliverances in three days at one conference alone. We assembled six teams of four people each, facilitating deliverances, one right after another. People were being set free and finding God in many different dimensions. After all these years I still run into people today who are walking in the freedom they gained at that time. The principles I learned were life giving, but I have beliefs that I have had to adjust over time.

Too many times, people assumed that in a prophetic deliverance ministry every strong woman had to be a Jezebel, and every weak man was stereotyped as an Ahab. I do believe those spirits exist and yes, where you're wounded, the enemy will come and exploit that area. But not every strong woman is a Jezebel, nor is every weak man an Ahab. This particular issue came very close to damaging my relationship with Susie. Did my wife need healing? Absolutely! Because of my all-encompassing devotion to leadership, I could have easily jeopardized my own family since I was taking time away from them to heal others.

This is a warning: The Lord Jesus Christ is your covering, and to Him you must pledge your allegiance. Yes, I understand that the husband covers his wife, but not at the expense of allowing either partner's destiny to be derailed. When I came into Sonship, I understood that the covering was taken care of by Father God. It was protection by relationship, not a covering that limited my ability to reach my full potential. When I stand before the Lord Jesus Christ, He will ask me this question, "Where are the wife and children I put you in charge of?" I will have to account for how I treated them, as well as how I ministered to other people.

Small groups can be places where genuine healing really comes. To quote James 5:16: *"Confess your trespasses one to another and pray for one another that you may be healed."* In the house church movement, this is done very well due to the continuing fellowship and relationship of the participants.

I can remember our criticisms of people in the church system who called themselves apostles. We would say, "They're not apostles; they are pastors on steroids." We thought we had the new revelation, and they didn't. During this time, Susie and I were having a crisis with our son Jason, who had graduated with a 4.0 average from Trinity Christian Academy. He is a very smart kid! Jason was experimenting with drugs; he loved to smoke pot and get high. He told us that he used to smoke pot almost every single day before he went to school. For many years, I'd begged the Lord to help me as a father to bring deliverance and healing to him. One night at about 3:00 a.m., when Jason was 16, the Lord showed me prophetically where he hid his drugs. He told me to wake him up, expose his drugs, put them on the counter, do a Bible teaching on mercy with him, and then demonstrate mercy by flushing the drugs down the toilet and never mention it again.

I can remember asking the Lord to judge Jason. See, I knew that he needed an encounter with the living God to break his addiction. I personally pleaded with God to judge him as God had judged me. When Jesus walked through the wall to me that night, He told me that if I did not choose Him, He would let hell have its way with me. That was judgment. It was judgment with mercy, because He knew that I was going to choose Him. It was not judgment of wrath! I was certain God could do it and that He could get through to Jason. I wasn't so sure that I could communicate with him that night. After all those years of dealing with the addictions in my life and my family, I had become religious, judgmental, and hardhearted. In some ways, I had become just like my father standing on his principles with an iron fist.

In spite of the drug use, Jason was a model son. He never broke curfew. He never skipped school, kept perfect grades, was respectful, loved sports, worked hard, and was by all accounts a great kid. He even told me one time that some of his friends asked why he always had money. He told them that he tithed, and therefore God took care of him financially. You might want to say that's bogus, but you know, Kingdom principles work for the just and the unjust.

Jason had graduated from high school and went to a junior college in North Florida. I can hear him now, "Finally, out from underneath the control of Mom and Dad, I can do what I want." Jason had a scholarship playing baseball and was writing for the school paper, but he started doing crack cocaine. It wasn't too long before we knew that he was in trouble. There was only one thing we could do, and that was to pray. For months, I had a demon spirit visit me every morning and tell me that Jason was going to die because of his drug use. Day after day after day, this spirit would torment me. I became convinced he would die. But thank God, one morning during prayer, my King broke through the noise of that tormenting spirit with a thundering voice. He told me, "Now that you have come into agreement with a demon, that Jason will die, are you at least man enough to preach his funeral and get his friends saved?" What a question! The Holy Spirit started to show me how I had come into agreement with this demonic spirit. With that revelation, I broke that covenant of agreement with the lie that Jason was going to die. I started to believe the promises that the Lord had given me many years ago. Then the Holy Spirit armed me with the Scripture that I have used to restore both of my sons at points of crisis in their lives:

I have been young, and now am old; yet I have not seen the righteous forsaken, nor his seed begging for bread. Psalms 37:25 (KJV)

Armed with this Scripture and the knowledge that God is a generational God, I started to do warfare on behalf of my children. I claimed the Godly legacy that I was supposed to leave them. I may still have been an orphan myself, but I had finally come to the revelation that I was righteous! Just because I am blessed with righteousness, doesn't allow my children the right to live a lifestyle that will put them into a place of a beggar, spiritually or naturally. God would provide the bread to nourish my sons.

All through Scripture, bread is symbolic of God's presence. I like the reference of the showbread in the Old Testament, which was behind the veil in the Holy Place. In his book, "God Chasers," Tommy Tenney taught me to call it the "show up bread." Any time you lean your heart toward His presence, the bread of His presence shows up.

In the book of Ruth, Elimelech and his wife Naomi were natives of Bethlehem, which means "House of Bread." There was a famine there, so they traveled to the land of Moab searching for sustenance. My sons, and thousands like them, are leaving, or have left the church system for the same reason. There is "no Bread of His presence." Now, Moab was a cruel place. It robbed Naomi of her spouse, and was the place she had to bury her sons. It will steal your dreams before their time, if you are not careful.

So, when I pray Psalms 37:25, *"I have been young and now am old, yet have I not seen the [uncompromisingly] righteous forsaken or his seed begging bread,"* (AMP) I decree that my sons will not lack His presence, no matter where they need to find it. When Naomi was at her lowest point, still in Moab, she heard a rumor that there was bread back in Bethlehem.

> *Then she arose with her daughters-in-law that she might return from the country of Moab, for she had heard in the country of Moab that the Lord had visited His people by giving them bread. Ruth 1:6*

The spirit of Moab does what he is allowed to do with our children. Since the devil is on a short leash, my sons' God-given destiny could be preserved through His presence. When our children hunger for the real Bread, they can find it. Most of us don't have His presence, and we can't give what we don't have.

Look at the prodigal son story in Luke 15. When the younger son became hungry, he came to his senses. When he came to his senses, he didn't go to the church. He went back to his father's house. But it wasn't the father's love for him—not even the robe, ring or sandals—that restored his identity; it was the celebration.

You will show me the path of life; In Your presence is fullness of joy; At Your right hand are pleasures forevermore.   Psalm 16:11

Let my vindication come from Your presence; Let Your eyes look on the things that are upright.   Psalm 17:2

Look what decreeing bread back into our children's lives brings… joy and vindication from the presence of God. It ushers in a party… not some hellfire and brimstone, Bible-thumping, mad parent. Our young people crave a party of God's presence; so wherever your child finds bread, go have a party with him and stop preaching.

As a mother with a child on crack, Susie was having her own crisis. She would tell me, "If you had not been so religious and dogmatic in your belief system, Jason would not have run to the drugs." In some ways, she was probably right. Jason went to school at Trinity Christian Academy, which was part of the church, and he saw all the corruption that had been going there. In reality, he had plenty of natural excuses to resist God. I remember, in the middle of a heated argument with Susie, I yelled back at her, "I might be a Jesus freak, but Jesus promised me, my family. Jesus promised to restore my marriage and my sons. And I'm standing on that promise." I can tell you that all hell will try to stop you from believing the promises that only God can pull off.

Months later I attended a Promise Keepers' meeting in Tampa, Florida. In the midst of 40,000 men, we were worshiping to the song, "For Me and My House, We Will Serve the Lord." I broke down and started weeping. I asked the Lord if I had sinned, and canceled God's ability to give me the promise of my son, and my family. My son was doing crack, and my wife was battling depression. I couldn't sing the song "For Me and My House, We Will Serve the Lord" because my home was fractured, and my house was broken.

The Lord assured me that I had been faithful. Then He spoke this to me, "Charlie, most of the men in this stadium do not know what it would cost them to be faithful to me. But you have been faithful. Go home and tell Susie to prepare the fatted calf. And tell her, Jason will not die." For years I'd asked God to judge Jason, so he could break his addiction, and the Lord said to me, "Charlie, I'm going to judge Jason." Since I had asked God to do this for years, you would've thought my response would be, "It's about time!" Instead, I started begging God to show him mercy! It was my father's heart being expressed. When God judges His children, His judgment is always laced with mercy, to draw us back to Him. There is a day allocated for the final judgment. I personally believe that day has already come and gone. It was the day they crucified Jesus. If Jesus took the sins of the world unto Himself, then the world no longer has a sin problem. It only has a revelation problem of who Jesus is, and what He did on the cross. If I am wrong and there is another day, then I am still covered. Until then, I will try to walk in love and power. I am not looking to be raptured from the earth. I am personally looking to take over the world as I bring heaven here daily. The problem is you can't bring heaven to earth, if you don't go to heaven!

I knew a preacher who asked if I believed in the rapture, and I said, "Why yes I do, I go to heaven at least three or four times a day." He didn't think that was funny, because he would not die to himself. He is waiting to escape, instead of planning to take over.

Kingdom Key:
Many times your best indicator of success is your enemy, not your friend.

I figured out how to tell Susie what God had said. The questions came running through our heads. "What does 'he won't die' mean?" she would ask. "Susie, it means God is getting ready to do something and that Jason will not die. I don't have any other answers, just believe with me," I would tell her. Ten days later Jason was partying in the Daytona Beach area with some of his old friends. At 4:00 in the morning, there was a knock on our front door. Jason's friend Matt was panicked! "Mr. Coker, Jason's in the front seat of the car, and he has passed out. He hasn't slept in days, and he's lost his mind. He has overdosed. The last coherent thing he told us to do was, 'Get me to my Daddy. He'll know what to do,' he shared through frightened tears."

We brought him into the house. I laid him on the couch with his head in my lap, and I started praying in the Spirit. Susie was telling me to take him to the hospital. "No, God said he would not die!" At 9:00 the next morning, Jason and I got on our knees. We completely surrendered our lives to the Lord Jesus Christ for the use of the Kingdom. We had a brief deliverance time. Before I left the house to go to work, I walked into the bedroom, and my wife had the covers pulled up over her head. She was surrendering to her depression.

As I sat on the bed, I spoke firmly, yet lovingly, "Susie, God didn't bring us this far to abandon us now. God has a plan. So get out of this bed, get your Bible out, do your devotions, figure out what that plan is, and do your part." As I was opening the store, the phone rang, and it was Susie who said, "You're not going to believe what my devotion was today." She opened her devotional for that morning, and the heading was 'God has a plan'."

Jason returned to college. A couple of weeks later he called me one day and said, "Dad, I had one of your crazy visions. In this vision God showed me how He's always had His hand on my baseball game, and He's going to take me to division one college ball. Dad, God says that He's going to pay for my school. God wants to use my baseball skills and has a purpose for my life!" he told me with a fresh joy in his voice that I had not heard for a long time.

It was great news that God was starting to speak to my son in visions about a given purpose, especially the part where God said He was going to pay for it. I had cut Jason off because of his drug abuse. God did have a plan, and thankfully, it wasn't going to cost me a cent!

Jason's friend Matt, who had brought him to the house that night, was playing baseball at Bethune-Cookman University in Daytona Beach. Jason wound up earning a scholarship to play baseball at an historical black college. (Sure glad I dealt with my racism!)

Several weeks later, I was in prayer at about three o'clock in the morning. The Lord asked me if I was willing to relinquish my responsibility as a father over Jason. I saw the position of authority, anointing, and the generational aspect of fathering, and now He was asking me to lay it on the altar for a season. He said that if I was willing to relinquish this position, He would bring another man into his life who would father him for a time and bring some healing to his wounds. When this season was over, God would hand him back to me.

Little did I know that Jason was walking by the science building and saw an inscription that read "all science points to God." He felt like the Lord told him to change his degree from business to religion and philosophy. As he walked into the religion and philosophy building, he ran into the department head, Dr. James Brooks. Later, when Dr. Brooks and I compared notes, the encounter we each had with the Holy Spirit occurred about the same time. While God was asking me if I was willing to relinquish my rights as a father over Jason, God was telling this African-American, well-educated, professor to treat Jason as a son. God used Dr. Brooks to bring the necessary healing to Jason that I could not. Jason played baseball and became the director of the Fellowship of Christian Athletes. We called him the token white boy at an historical black college.

Jason finished his four years of college and earned a degree in religion and philosophy. Thanks to Dr. Brooks' influence, he proceeded to attend Oral Roberts University, and earned a master's degree in Biblical literature. My willingness to let another man father my son in the areas of my weakness came back to me full circle in business, when Jason fathered me for a season and ran the business instead of me.

After Jason married and graduated from Oral Roberts University, he moved back to the area. We set up a deliverance session for him and his wife. Because he was my son, I was asked not to be on the team; I simply sat in the next room and interceded for them both. As Apostle Tim led the deliverance session, the rest of the team could not catch the curse that was on Jason. Tim asked Jason for my help, because he wanted an outside confirmation of the vision God showed him.

To my surprise, when Tim asked me what curse was on him, I blurted out, "A 'bastard curse'!" The vision that God had shown him was my mother-in-law walking up to Jason when he was born in the hospital, grabbing his little toes and saying, "You're a bastard." At that spoken word, a demon was assigned to Jason to fulfill that curse. This didn't seem fair. I married his mother, and I became his father. The bottom line was, Jason was conceived outside of a marriage covenant. Even though eventually we did what was right, I did not deal with this curse at the time. The curse was upon my son from the day he was conceived.

> *A bastard shall not enter into the congregation of the Lord; even to his tenth generation shall he not enter into the congregation of the Lord. Deuteronomy. 23:2*

Once this curse was broken, Jason and I became best friends. Doors opened for us to do business and ministry together. For the first time with this curse broken, we started to become family at a heart level.

I've told this story and have used it as an illustration for altar calls as I've traveled and preached. I'm totally shocked by how many people come to have this curse broken off of them. I've seen grandmas bring children up. I've seen as many as 50% of a congregation come to the altar in one service. The blood of Jesus and the cross cancel the curse, but we have to enforce the power of the blood to redeem our inheritance.

An apostle works from the foundation of the pyramid to lift people up spiritually. This is truly how this model needs to function. When people see a beautiful mansion, they gush over the furniture, the lovely columns, the walls and windows, yet few even notice the foundation. The structure needed to support the mansion and everything in it is usually covered by dirt. How was it even possible to build the foundation in rocky soil? Of course, dynamite was used to blow out the boulders and root systems to make the foundation as strong as could be. I believe that's the purpose of the deliverance ministry. It digs down deep into the lives of God's people to blow out the rocks, roots, and generational sins. With the removal of these things, there's a foundation on which to build something unbreakable that symbolizes the Kingdom. This foundation is an absolute necessity for true Kingdom life!

During this time, one of my spiritual sons, who had worked for me and been under my wing for years, went to work for a very large ministry in Orlando. Through his relationships with the ministry, he formed a company, which generated tremendous income for people who were supporting many ministries. Making a long story short, we started working together and for several years were pouring tens of thousands of dollars back into ministry. I had become the anointed businessman who brought finances to the ministry. I saw this as the wealth of the wicked stored up for the righteous.

If you've ever seen the TV show, "Deadliest Catch" on the Discovery Channel, it's easy to understand. When the guys are catching pots full of crab, the captain is a hero, but once the pots start coming up empty, everyone's out for the captain's head. Needless to say, what we thought was the Holy Ghost gravy train was about to come to a screeching halt. I went from being a Joseph in Potiphar's house to a demonic security breach in one phone call.

On a trip to New York, while hanging out with Apostle Tim, I told him that I believed the Lord had shown me that I was one of the keys to revival in America. I had visions about the coming move of God. I'd seen my mother's prayers and a vision had shown my mother walking up the hill praying about the end time harvest and envisioning the glory cloud of God saving, healing, and delivering people, all at the same time. This encounter left an imprint on my spirit that still drives me to His presence today. As I shared the intimate details of what I believed the Lord had shown me, I did not know that Tim believed I was arrogant even as I was speaking the words.

The next day, the phone rang with dreadful news, a call that no one ever wants. My business partner informed me, "The FBI has come to the office and has seized all of our assets. You need to get on a plane and come home!" That night, I rented a room at the Hampton Inn in Rochester, New York waiting for a flight out the next morning. My mind was spinning, what had gone wrong? Had this truly been a Ponzi scheme? In my heart I cried out, "Oh God, I have to face all of our investors! God,

I asked if this is You. God, I have my life savings in this! God, we have $5.1 million tied up! God, am I going to jail? God, You know my heart!"

When I get into a situation where I need to really hear God, and can't get alone in the woods or in my car, I love to take long hot showers. So, I took a long hot shower in my room at the hotel. I didn't know what I was going to face the next day with the FBI. Things were so out of my control that I stayed in the shower too long, and my body started to overheat. I can remember it as if it was yesterday. A spirit of suicide came into that bathroom, and spoke to me. It hissed, "If you'll stay in the shower just a little longer, when they find your body, they will think it was an accident." I had battled the spirit of suicide earlier in my life but that voice came from the inside. This time, I heard it from the outside; recognizing that, I looked at this spirit, and answered back, "It's only a few million dollars and my reputation. What's the big deal?"

That visitation with the spirit of suicide actually empowered me to know that God had a bigger plan for me. I knew that the devil, the father of lies, was trying to get me to take myself out, so I wouldn't be in position to plunder the kingdom of darkness. The devil tried to push my buttons, "What if you go to jail?" I told the devil, that Paul wrote some of his best books of the Bible in jail, and I knew that God had told me I would write books one day.

I begged God for the strength to man up and face the music. I realized that we HAD been involved in a $160 million Ponzi scheme. We lost all our finances and assets… seemingly everything. This was probably the most critical emotional crisis that we had faced as a family in ten years. With one phone call, my reputation was gone and my company was in jeopardy. I feared going to jail. It was overwhelming.

I can tell you that my heart was pure, but the people we were connected to were wrong. My intentions were to financially support ministry, and we did. The Kingdom principal I learned was: " You can lose your reputation and still have your integrity."

In the midst of this, I felt word curses coming from people I trusted. They weren't just words from investors and friends who had been hurt and confused by all this, but there was a demonic assault in these curses from a hidden source. So one night I prayed, "Lord, I need to figure out how to battle this, and where it's coming from." I went into a prophetic vision. In this vision I went back in time, into the dining room of Apostle Tim's home during Thanksgiving dinner. Because of the call about the FBI, I had flown home the day before. I listened as Tim told everyone who was there, including people with whom I had been connected spiritually, that I had become a security breach. He claimed it was because of my arrogance and pride. "Who was I to think that I was a key to revival?" God exposed the word curses to me that evening! The words of the elderly gentleman were shown to be true, that Tim would use me as long as I was useful.

After this prophetic encounter, I started asking the Lord what was going on. Only a major crisis like that could force me to open my eyes and to get me to leave the apostolic system I was pursuing. It felt as if the apostolic ministry, that I believed would usher in this great end time harvest, had betrayed me.

I carried the information from the prophetic encounter for over three months and shared it with no one. One day I got Apostle Tim in my vehicle and pulled off on a dirt road. (I wanted to shoot him, but King Jesus wouldn't let me). I told him about the encounter I had, and what God had shown me. Tim started tearing up and asking me to forgive him! He appeared to be totally astonished. God had just given him the revelation as we spoke, that I was petrified to stand in the pulpit and preach. His assumption that I was arrogant and prideful was wrong. I was simply too afraid and insecure to move into another realm of gifting.

Needless to say, I was battling major depression and hopelessness, since everything I had worked for was gone. I had jeopardized my entire family and my company. My ministry reputation was toast, and yeah, I went into a deep depression. Most people assumed my depression was because of the financial losses. I do have to admit it definitely had a part to play, but my biggest sadness was that I had put my whole heart into the apostolic system. I truly believed I would be doing ministry with these people until the day I met Jesus face to face. (I'm one of those all-in guys). When we don't know who we are as sons, we battle fears and insecurities. When we lack maturity, we have a tendency to look for the approval of others to validate our calling. When we do this, we are opening ourselves to be misread and often misjudged. Sad to say, the relationship between us never recovered.

God sent me to a church in Daytona while I was still building ministry in the house church movement with Apostle Tim. Pastor Rodney* led this church. He is an apostle, and his wife Kathy is a prophet. They're connected with Bishop Bill Hammond. I saw the apostolic and prophetic work hand-in-hand between them. The first time that I went to one of their meetings, the Lord give me a word to release to the church. Unsure, I told the Lord that if He wanted me to release the word that He needed to speak to the authority in the house. Pastor Kathy prophetically called me out and said, "God told you to give a word. Why didn't you release it?" So, I went forward and gave the word. The following week I returned and the same thing happened. She rebuked me again for not releasing the word God had given me. It became obvious between us, that they knew who I was by the Spirit, and we started building a relationship.

For a year or so, I was part of this church and observed how the apostle and prophet worked together. I saw traces of the old wineskins of the church system, but also saw the apostolic working as the foundational triangle. This was a great time of healing for me. I was received as a prophet, released to do ministry, and thrived in the environment.

Apostle Rodney called me to his office one day, and on the ride over, I said to Susie, "I have been to these kinds of meetings before, so I'm not sure what to expect today." To my surprise, what I saw was truly triangle-point-down-pushing-up-fathering.

Rodney and Kathy asked me how I was doing, told me I had been at the church for over a year, and asked if I felt healed and ready to do what I was called to do. Rodney let me know that he recognized that I was not simply a house prophet, and he wanted me to start traveling again. I needed to stop hanging around the church, because when I showed up, I brought unrest to what he was trying to accomplish. The regional gifting was not being used properly, and I was bringing unrest to the whole house. He said to check in, give testimony, and begin to travel again to fulfill my destiny. This was a breath of fresh air. I wasn't asked to leave; I was told to go do what I was called to do. When I stand before the Lord Jesus Christ, He will ask me this question, "Where are the wife and children I put you in charge of?" I can honestly say, "They are doing great!

Kingdom Keys:

1. You can lose your reputation and still have integrity.

2. If you cannot love by your standards, you cannot live by them either.

3. Remember the cross and the blood of Jesus cancels all curses.

4. All hell will try to stop you from believing the promises that only God can pull off. Stand firm in His promises always.

5. Many times your best indicator of success is your enemy and not your friend.

Round 9

Who's in Charge, Father or Son?

About the time you think you have a handle on the revelation that the Lord has given you, He has a habit of testing you to see if you're willing to obey His principles. I remember the phone calls I received from my son Jason, who was living in Tulsa, Oklahoma, and finishing his degree in Biblical literature. The phone calls often went something like this, "Dad, the Lord has revealed to me that I'm supposed to come and work for you." Usually I would fire back, "Jason, it's not God. You have a degree in Bible, and now you're going to sell light bulbs for me? No." Click.

Ring, ring: "Dad, listen to me. God has told me that I'm supposed to move home and work for you at the store." "Jason, I don't believe it's God. You have a degree in Bible, and you wanted to further your education." Click!

Ring, ring: "Dad, don't hang up on me. Listen to me! I know it's God, and I am coming to go to work for you. You need me, and I'm coming to do that." "Jason, are you sure this is God? If it is, we'll work out the details."

I can hear you asking, why would a father make it so difficult for a son to tell what God had shown him? I was slow to receive him, because I knew that working for me would be very difficult. If he wasn't 100% sure it was God, there would not be grace enough for him to survive. I did it because when it got tough and he wanted to quit, he would know God had sent him. I can't tell you the hell that we went through, learning the process of the apostolic inverted triangle model, or the idiosyncrasies of running a family business that was in financial crisis. Add to that three strong personalities and you have a recipe for disaster. I already had a manager when Jason came to work with me, so for his first two years at the lighting store, Jason had to submit to both the manager and me. It's difficult running a family business, because there are so many different hats to wear. Some days you don't know if you are wearing the hat of the business owner, father, boss, or even husband, because your wife is keeping the books. (I have learned this axiom firsthand: if Momma ain't happy, ain't nobody happy!)

I can remember one day Susie and I got into an argument at the store about something she had done. Man, did we get into a fight! The whole place knew that we were fighting. The next morning my manager shrugged and asked, "Dude, I know God healed your marriage, but after yesterday's fight, my question is why?" I said, "That is a funny question coming from somebody who almost lost his marriage, because his communication skills are so poor. You can't even tell your wife how you really feel." My manager looked at me with a deer in the headlights expression. "Listen, Susie and I believe in the kingdom principle, 'don't let the sun go down on your wrath.' We fixed it before we went to bed, and actually were romantic last night."

Years ago, a Christian counselor told me my marriage would never succeed, but we're still here. So, I have a hard time hearing advice from people who have been divorced three or four times. I am teachable, and I definitely need help. I don't know many people who have restored a broken marriage like ours. Susie and I will explain our story in detail in our book called, "From Rape to Righteousness, Redeeming the Bride of Christ."

After a couple of years, Jason came to me and said he had made a decision. He wanted a place within the company. So, he sat me down with a business plan and laid it out. As I was reviewing his business plan and his proposals, the Holy Spirit started speaking to me about this apostolic triangle being the foundation of everything, even my business. I believe that the apostolic carries the fathering mantle for the Kingdom. The Lord started speaking to me about giving Jason complete control over the company. He said that Jason was a much better businessman than I was. I'm a great salesman—that's my strength in business. My own orphan spirit and insecurities only emphasized my weaknesses. I've needed someone to cover those weaknesses, so I've always had partners. I gave up a lot of my authority to the other people, allowing others to fill in for me in the weak places, instead of leading as I was called to do.

The Lord ordered me to give Jason complete control over the company. He was to have all the assets at his disposal to run it as he saw fit. I had been my own boss for over 25 years. Susie and I had weathered multiple storms, and we had always come out on top. It had always been "us against the world." Now, God was asking me to give control of my company to a 24-year-old kid. It sure was a big blow to my ego! I didn't know then that God was trying to teach me how the apostolic works in real life and not just in theory. If you look at Scripture, you'll find that Jesus did not start performing miracles, which expanded the Kingdom, until God the Father audibly spoke a blessing for all to hear:

> *When all the people were baptized, it came to pass that Jesus also was baptized; and while He prayed, the heaven was opened. And the Holy Spirit descended in bodily form like a dove upon Him, and a voice came from heaven which said, "You are My beloved Son; in You I am well pleased." Luke 3:21*

The Lord was teaching me the power of a father's blessing which releases the true identity into the son. God was leading me to empower Jason with my blessing, sending the message that if you do business with Jason, you are doing business with me.

According to tradition, that's what a Jewish father would do in the middle of the town square. He would present his son, who was his apprentice in training. Publicly, he would declare his approval of his son. In doing so, he was telling the town "from now on if you do business with my son, you are also doing business with me. He has full authority to do the family business."

When Jesus was 12 years old, He tried to explain to Mary that He had been granted the Father's authority, but did not have the maturity for favor from man. He was still under the authority of his parents. When we begin to come into our true understanding of God, the Father, our Sonship is revealed. He will also anoint us to do business on His behalf, by the power of His blessing. 1 Peter 3:9 puts it this way: *...Not returning evil for evil or reviling for reviling, but on the contrary blessing, knowing that you were called to this, that you may inherit a blessing.* Blessings have tremendous power to cancel evil and position you to inherit a blessing! God's blessing on you is much greater than a public validation of a father toward his son.

One of the first hurdles we had to overcome was when Jason decided to fire his brother Bryan. This was made a little easier because the day he fired Bryan, I had asked an electrician friend of mine if he would hire him. So Jason fired him, and gave him a job at the same time.

The next decision was a little more difficult. Jason said to me, "Dad, you and Mom have made a living, but this is a mom-and-pop shop. If we are ever going to be a real company, we have to fire Mom." Jason knew we needed different skills than my wife possessed, but telling her was the scariest thing we ever had to do. (I told Jason that he had to do it, because I close both eyes when I sleep!) You have to remember, Susie was the warehouse girl when the employees were sick, and she worked nights if necessary… she filled any gap. When we presented it to her at first, she was a little upset. She felt as if we were pushing her out of the company. What we were really doing was turning control over to Jason, so he could manage differently. As it worked out, she continued to work at the company. Jason took control of paying the bills, and setting budgets, and she worked beside him. Truth be known, he took most of the pressure that she'd been carrying from her. Once Jason made a decision, it was his way or the highway. I sure was glad it worked out; I have to live with her!

Several years earlier I complained to the Lord about Susie. I told God I didn't think she was spiritual enough. The Lord told me to go ask her about the condition of the company checkbook. When I did, she asked me to come into agreement with her in prayer, to believe that God would bring in $5000 by Friday to pay the current bills. So we prayed.

As I left the office that day the Lord let me know, "Susie is using her faith to bring in the finances for this company to survive. Do not question her spiritual condition by your gifting. Your ways are not My ways. You need to be more sensitive with her. She was my daughter before she was your wife." A few years later, after Jason and I had rapidly opened new branches, I complained about Susie's spiritual condition again. The Lord spoke to me "Go ask her about the condition of the company checkbook." She said, "It's not a big deal. I'm just believing God to bring in $96,000 by Friday, so I can cover these checks that I have written." I guess her faith had grown!

Running a business with Kingdom principles is a difficult thing to do with several strong personalities involved. I was challenged because God had put Jason in control. I had to be sure that I was hearing God when I spoke, and then be patient, giving others time to respond or not. This was a very difficult lesson for me. There was a carpet store next door, and we shared a warehouse. One day they overheard Jason and me arguing. The TV show, "Orange County Choppers," where Paul, Sr., and Paul, Jr. yell, scream, cuss and throw things, was a pretty good representation of our arguments, without the cussing… sometimes. They started screaming back, "Hey Pauly," and mocking us like the TV show.

I went to the Lord and asked how we could communicate and make this work. Lord said to me, "The issue is your lack of honor of his gifting. If you will honor his gifting, he will in turn honor yours. Then you will be on the same page." One of the Kingdom principles that God has taught me is, "You cannot have what you don't honor." The picture on the next page was hung in an office that Jason and I shared. When you looked at my desk and then his, it makes sense. Just remember the boats got tied up on both sides of the dock.

About this time, I was working mostly in the office where my spiritual son and I were doing the joint ventures business, not at the lighting store. But when that Ponzi scheme blew up in my face, the whole family and business were put into a major crisis. With the crisis at hand, Jason just cut my salary in half, fired half of our staff, and made the company lean and mean, so we could become profitable quickly.

Honoring The Gifting of Others takes Love and Patience

Jason had become totally focused on money and the condition of the company. Under that stress he lacked sensitivity in the area of my personal finances and had become what Susie called, "Mr. Pissy Pants." One day I was about to let him have it and the Lord said, "He is your authority. Submit to him with the right attitude, and I will give you favor with your boss." I have to tell you that was a little hard to take. Technically I owned the whole company, I was this kid's father, and I believed I could kick his butt.

The Lord said I was only right on one of the three counts. Number one: the Lord said He owned the company, because I had given it to Him. Number two: I **was** Jason's father. Number three: Jason would probably win in a fistfight. So the Lord said to me, "Why don't you sit down and speak to him like a father and not a disgruntled employee? If you have any complaints, remember you raised this boy."

Under Jason's leadership, we started functioning as a well-oiled machine. God would give me a vision or speak to me in a word. I would present it to Jason. He would then process it totally differently than I did. But every time we would come to the same conclusion; the Lord was telling us to expand, or make major business decisions. When I honored his gifting, gave him time, and space, he would always come to the conclusion that I already had. The great part about Jason was that he not only came to the same conclusion, he came with a blueprint on how to execute it.

During this season I learned how to communicate with Jason and teach him people skills that he sorely lacked. He was a black-and-white, nuts and bolts, by the numbers administrator. So I fathered him over coffee, on a drive to one of our branches, or on different projects that we worked on together. Jason allowed me to father him in the area of his weaknesses. This was the most fruitful season of my life with my son. He'd become my best friend, my business partner, and he took care of my administrative issues for the ministry.

God has shown me the blueprint of the apostolic ministry in the church. A spiritual father, still in his prime, gives control to his son, submits to him, and pushes him to the top.

I can remember manufacturers' reps with whom I had done business for 20 years coming to me and saying, "Hey, Jason is no longer buying my product." I would tell them that Jason had made the decision because their pricing was not right, or they didn't have the right product. They would say to me, "Aren't you the owner? Don't you make these decisions? We've done business for 20 years." I had to tell them, "I may be the owner on paper, but Jason is the boss. If Jason says, 'No, it's no.' You haven't earned his business."

Jason became the golden boy in our industry because our company began to thrive under his leadership. One of the old-time reps came back from the Dallas market with a story that I've pondered in my heart for years. A bunch of businesspeople were talking about our company, and how Jason had turned the company around. They were bragging about how competent Jason was and his good business decisions, and rightly so. But this old rep said something interesting. He said, "You know, I've been around a bit longer than some of you guys. I can remember when

Charlie Coker was on the back stoop of his business, praying that God would deliver that boy from drugs. Charlie told me that one day God was going to deliver him, and he would be in business and ministry with him." One of the other reps at the table, who knew me very well, made a joke and said, "Charlie surely does pray a lot. I tried to pray the other morning, but God put me on hold and told me He was on the phone with Charlie. I'd have to wait."

As I'm writing this chapter I'm thinking about all of the principles of the Kingdom the Lord has taught me through my business, and all the people that I have affected.

What I've learned about businessmen is that they are kings. When you look at Scripture, the king went, did business, and provided resources for the priest to do his job. I believe the church system has a tendency to rate the businessman for his finances and not for his spirituality, wisdom, and his entrepreneurial gifting. I see that one of the reasons why the church is so weak is because we've elevated the priesthood, and devalued the businessman, and his spiritual effectiveness within our communities.

During this season, the Lord had already convinced me that I walked in the office of a prophet. He was also telling me that I was an Apostle. He started waking me up at 4:48 every morning until I submitted to that call:

Then Jesus said to him, "Unless you people see signs and wonders, you will by no means believe." John 4:48

Truly the signs of an apostle were accomplished among you with all perseverance, in signs and wonders and mighty deeds. 2 Corinthians 12:12

I asked the Lord, "If the Scripture is true, what does the function of a modern-day apostle look like?"

So the next morning, He sent me to a coffee shop in town owned by a Christian businessman I knew. As I got my coffee and sat down at the table, the Holy Spirit asked me if I thought I was an Apostle. I replied, "You said I was, and therefore I must be." At that point He told me that I carry the government of the Kingdom upon my life as an apostle. Wade, the business owner, was in desperate need of $1000 to pay his coffee bill, or he would not be able to do business. (Everybody wants to hear God better, unless it costs them.) Previously, that wouldn't have been a problem. I would have written a check or used a credit card. Now I was under a mandate to submit all financial giving to Jason and my wife, because I had a habit of giving away the farm and then putting God's name on it.

So God had just painted me into a corner. What a pickle! I asked the Lord, "As an apostle and a government official of the Kingdom, what do I do?" He said to declare and to decree $1000 to show up in my hands, so I could give it to Wade. So I started praying under my breath; I started whispering and decreeing that $1000 would manifest and show up. Then I could do what I was called to do as a government official of the Kingdom. I was on my third hour there, my eighth cup of coffee, and was getting disgusted with this training program God put me in. I closed my eyes and visualized God the Father handing me $1000, so I could give it to one of His other sons.

At that point, my friend Roger walked through the door. Roger got his coffee and sat down at my table. I said to him, "Glad you finally obeyed God, and came to bring me my $1000," Roger asks, "What $1000?" I looked Roger in the eyes and said, "Where is my money?" He started laughing and asked, "How did you know I had this check for you?" Roger had written a check 3 days earlier for $1000, made out to my ministry. With that, we called Wade over to the table. I told Wade what God had shown me. I signed the check over to him. He started to weep. He told us that he'd been in the office asking God for the money to pay his coffee bill, so he could stay in business.

Training that I would need in order to understand how government in the Kingdom really works had begun. We need to be able to take responsibility for the sins of the past and have a clear vision of the Kingdom of the future in order to have authority in cities, businesses, churches and regions.

I began to get a clearer understanding of how God was teaching me through my business. I saw that the Kingdom functions with heavenly mandates and the blueprints of heaven manifest on earth through His fivefold ministry.

As I look back, I see that the lighting showroom we built in St Augustine, near Jacksonville, was a complete stretch of faith at the time. God told us to build a new showroom with a design center. He also said to shift our business plan, so we could do more lighting design and not be limited to national builders' accounts. It had been over 20 years since I had done high-end design work. It's like the Lord said, "You build it, and they will come." This particular showroom was 20 miles south of Jacksonville. Two weeks before we were going to open, I met Steve who had been an owner of one of the largest lighting showrooms in Florida. The high-end design market was his area of expertise. When I met him, I immediately saw the Holy Spirit on his life. I also saw the brokenness God had led him through. He had recently been driven out of the company that he had owned and built for over 30 years. He was now working out of an office with an electrician, 150 yards from this new showroom. To make a long story short, we became partners; his skills meshed perfectly within our design center.

During our relationship, I had to continue to remind him not to be bitter and angry with his ex-partner over the loss of his company. When his ex-partner's firm went bankrupt, we were able to purchase the legal name and the inventory of his old company.

I remember the day I had a meltdown working in a warehouse trying to load trucks and salvage the inventory. I was staying in Jacksonville working like a dog, 18 hours a day. I went to the showroom where Steve was meeting with a guy who had money to invest in the rebirth of the old company. He was a believer also. He was needed in our company because he could write big checks. I felt like a "dirtball" and was very angry over the whole situation. I remember the Lord showing up in the corner of the warehouse. He started to speak to me. He told me that He was very proud that I was willing to do my part in redeeming a brother's inheritance that had been lost. He showed me that the day was coming when I would not only do the labor part but also write the checks to help redeem the sons of God's inheritance.

When Jason and I decided to close the business, Steve and his partner took over that location and then reopened a store in the Jacksonville area. When you do business with the Kingdom in mind, God will use you to help restore to others what they lost, relationally, financially, and spiritually.

Here's an example of how you know your employees have figured out that you and God have a covenant relationship in business. One day my manager slammed down the phone and said, "If God owns this company, tell Him that He is on credit hold with Golden Lighting. They are not sending any more product until He sends them a check!" I remember God telling me I could use my faith or my credit, but that if I continued to use credit, He would get none of the credit that He rightly deserved. He was trying to teach me how to push and make something happen by faith, rather than by my own striving.

Kingdom Key:
If you always use YOUR credit, God will never get HIS credit.

I can tell you it was very satisfying doing ministry for years. I was going to New York once a month, learning how the Kingdom functions. I was able to pay my own way, so if the offering was small, it didn't matter. I believe the apostle Paul set the stage for businessmen to function as apostles in the marketplace.

While I was writing this chapter, Tony Cote, one of my former employees just happened to text me out of the blue that he "loved me." I don't think that was a coincidence. I called him, and told him that I was just explaining how in business, people's lives are impacted to expand the Kingdom. He let me know that I had been a great role model for him because I taught him how the prophetic worked. The timing of his message shocked both of us! God is so cool!

God asked me to start traveling back to New York again. I felt like

I had taken two different missionary trips: one with the church system, triangle point up; and the other with the apostolic house church system triangle point down. I had some success bringing unity between the two. In some cases, the only unity was that everyone was united in disagreement with me!

I let God know if I went back to New York, I expected to witness power as demonstrated in the book of Acts, or I was not wasting my time. He then reminded me of the Rolex watch He had promised me as a sign of this revival. My wife and Jason had given me a Tag Heuer watch worth about $1600. It was a nice watch, but not a Rolex! As the date was getting closer to travel again, I started to crank up the prayers. As I prayed, the Lord told me to connect with different people; to rebuild old relationships, and to form new ones. I wondered if my return to New York could be a sign that the Lord was promoting me in the Kingdom. Before, every time there was a promotion in the Spirit, it came after some form of death cycle. I had certainly been killed the last time I was in New York, if you remember! Jesus said it this way in John12: 23-26:

> *But Jesus answered them, saying, "The hour has come that the Son of Man should be glorified. Most assuredly, I say to you, unless a grain of wheat falls into the ground and dies, it remains alone; but if it dies, it produces much grain. He who loves his life will lose it, and he who hates his life in this world will keep it for eternal life. If anyone serves Me, let him follow Me; and where I am, there My servant will be also. If anyone serves Me, him My Father will honor.*

With Jesus as our example, God tries to put His glory upon us as sons. The process of death, burial, and resurrection is the same for us as it was for Jesus, the Only Begotten Son. Most of the time we run from every death process that God puts before us. We even call it demonic. Some of the time, it is actually God trying to kill our flesh and our worldly attitudes. Many times, God moving us from one position of authority to a greater position of authority, requires a separation from those with whom we have covenant. Often, a re-evaluation of the covenants with the people with whom you've walked in the last season is needed. The covenant between you and God is the highest covenant of all. The second covenant is between you and your spouse. Many people have been born again, but their covenant was with the church and not the living God. So when the church crumbles, they crumble with it.

You might think as I write this that I know what I'm doing, but let me tell you, I haven't had a clue many times. I am just now understanding that this has been a journey and a process. Please don't use the last statement as an excuse to walk in rebellion, manipulation, or in the spirit of accusation against the authority figures to whom God has told you to submit. As God kept prompting me to start traveling again to New York, I definitely had an attitude, and did not want to deal with the root issues in my heart. To be honest, I could have cared less about relationships at this point. All I wanted was revival, in spite of what God wanted. As I kept pushing God, He started to rebuke me for my attitude. He kept telling me that I was pushing Him out of His timing and that I needed to be patient, and do ministry His way, in His timing.

One morning God spoke to me about timing, and He asked if I wanted the Rolex He had promised. "Yes, I sure do! It is a sign for the timing of revival. That's what I've been looking for," I replied. He told me to give my Tag to Anthony, one of my employees. I let Susie and Jason know what God told me about giving Anthony my watch. I asked them for permission, because they were my authority in giving. I asked God to confirm the time for me to give Anthony his gift. The following week Anthony, Jason, and I were going to the Dallas lighting show. As we were walking down the jet way into the airplane, Anthony looked at Jason and me and said, "Wow, I'm going to the lighting show with the bosses! I need to look sharp, and I probably need to buy a new watch." Jason looked at me and said, "Redneck, there's your sign. Give your watch to Anthony." I explained to Anthony what all this meant. I told him about God's promise back in 1996 about giving me a Rolex, as the sign of revival coming. He received the gift with gladness.

We spent three nights in Dallas, and arrived home late Saturday night. I woke up early Sunday morning and started my prayers off with my demand list. I was telling God what I expected the next weekend in New York. God abruptly interrupted me. He was not very happy with me. In fact, He yelled at me, "Who do you think you're talking to?" At that point, I knew I had entered into the dead man's zone with God. He informed me that He did not want to hear my prayers any longer. He reminded me of an African-American pastor, Ricky, who had a church in Sanford, Florida. I had been in several meetings with him in the last few months and man, could he pray! He would pray and the atmosphere changed. God then gave me very clear instructions. I was to go by the office, get a company check for $300, go find Ricky's church that morning and give him my prayer list. He didn't want to hear me speak to Him any longer. He was ticked off. I did as I was told. I looked in the phone book and found Ricky's church in Sanford and drove about 30 minutes to attend his church service.

As I came into the building, Pastor Ricky recognized me and was honored that I would come. He handed me the microphone, and asked me to share with the people. I told them I got in trouble with God that morning, because I treated the Father like a waiter with all my demands. I told the group that the Father told me to bring a check for $300, and to give this church my prayer list. He didn't want to hear from me any longer. I then proceeded to prophesy over everyone in the building. As I finished prophesying, Ricky took the microphone and spoke, "As You were praying for my people, the Lord told me to give you my Rolex watch."

I was so amazed. God had replaced my watch and given me a Rolex in four days! I called my wife and son on the way home. I was rejoicing, giving God praise all the way. Once I got home, I started really studying the watch, and realized that it was not a blue-face Submariner, but a fake. It was fake, fake, fake!

As I sat in amazement, I asked God why He would give me a fake Rolex. God abruptly told me because of my attitude and my unwillingness to submit to His process. He warned me that with my attitude I was about to go birth a fake revival just like I got a fake Rolex. He then gave me instructions that I was not allowed to take this watch off my arm, until it fell off. You cannot believe the humility of wearing a fake Rolex. I scraped it up, and beat it against the concrete. I didn't want anyone to know that I had a fake Rolex.

That stinking thing turned green on my arm. Every day God continuously spoke to me, "You want to do it my way and have a real move of my Spirit, or do you want to have a fake revival that you'll have to sustain by yourself?" He then said to me, "You've been asking for breakthrough anointing, but you have refused to let Me break you."

Kingdom key:
To have a breakthrough anointing, you must be broken first.

I started having encounters with the Holy Spirit; He showed me what kind of ruler I was to become over the cities where I had been given responsibility. There was a prophet who was traveling around Hornell, New York, and the surrounding areas. I was receiving some unfavorable reports about his personal behavior, but the spiritual reports were that he was extremely prophetic, could hear the voice of God, and many said he reminded them of my ministry style and me.

I got a phone call from my 19-year-old niece. She started telling me about how a prophet called her out and gave her a prophecy almost word for word the same as one I had given her. Then she explained that this 60 year old man was not married, but he asked her to travel with him and do ministry. That was the final straw. I'd heard all the rumors, but those were all rumors. After I gave my niece very specific instructions, that she was not to travel with this man, and to avoid him at all costs, I started to pray.

Three days later in my morning prayers, the Lord asked this question, "How long are you going to tolerate this man's behavior in the city where I have given you responsibility?" He gave me clear instructions to confront him and tell him to leave. Responsibility will cost you! I told the Lord, "This is not something you do over a cell phone." I was willing to get on an airplane and confront him. God spoke, "Since you're willing, be patient. I'll tell you what to do, and what to say."

Two days later I got a phone call from this man. He was in Orlando, and wanted to come by my office. As we spoke, he told me he'd heard that I was a great prophet and had great gifting. He wanted us to do a conference together. With that invitation, I told him I would never share a pulpit with him. I explained why, with some inside information from the Lord, and told him never to set foot in my city again. Five years later, the Lord asked me, "What kind of leader are you?" The Lord sent me back to this man and asked me to try to bring reconciliation between him and several pastors in the city. I set up the meeting but he never showed up…

Kingdom keys:

1. You can't have what you won't honor.

2. You can be a foundation to others and submit to their authority.

3. Don't judge the spirituality of others by your own gifting.

4. Don't let the sun go down on your wrath (and don't go to bed angry with your spouse.)

5. The Kingdom looks for ways to restore what was lost.

6. If you always use YOUR credit, God will never get HIS credit.

7. To have a breakthrough anointing, you must be broken first.

Kingdom Authority

Round 10

The Younger Brother!

You've already read about the education God gave me through my business, and how He used my oldest son to teach me the Kingdom. I had no idea how God was going to use my younger son, Bryan. Of my two sons, Bryan is most like me. We both had a hard time with school, but have overcome it. We both love people, and loved being the life of the party. Bryan, like his daddy, loves racecars and speed. He had a little four-cylinder turbocharged Nissan that would absolutely fly. He would go to the racetrack, or rebuild cars in my garage. He had one car for racing and another he drove around town every day. He had become a motor head, like I was in my teen years.

When he left to begin living on his own, he decided to move his girlfriend in with him, and they started playing house. Susie and I watched Bryan pull away from us as a family. We saw that things were definitely wrong in his life, and it was getting critical. This girl was absolutely demonic. I can still hear Susie starting to fret, "Oh Lord, if she gets pregnant, we will have to put up with her. If she gets pregnant, she will ruin Bryan's life." The Lord prompted me to do the same thing with Bryan that I had with Jason. I started praying Psalms 37:25; but this time I prayed that he could keep his seed, and it not be planted in the belly of the enemy's camp. I was waiting for the timing to be right. If I am like my Daddy God, I have to look for the right timing.

When I choose the proper time, I will judge uprightly. Psalm 75:2

Many years ago the Holy Spirit was dealing with me about Susie and the things she was doing that I considered SIN. I was being very dogmatic about my convictions. He gave me a rhema word. I know it's taken out of context but it has worked for me.

> *Do not be rash with your mouth, And let not your heart utter anything hastily before God. For God is in heaven, and you on earth; Therefore let your words be few. Ecclessiates 5:2*

God told me that I am not the sin police, and that what Susie was doing wasn't sin, until He called it sin. He then told me to, "shut up and love her." If the window of His longsuffering closed, He would let me know. Until then the standard is love.

My whole family had begun to get really ticked off with me when I pushed my weight around in the Spirit realm. With the Holy Spirit's help, I had recovered a very broken marriage and a kid on crack, so why not now? Sometimes, you get tired of being mocked and made fun of by your whole family. I wonder if hell was trying to have its way with me. It's harder to re-establish something that never should have been broken in the first place. If God had let me, I would have started over, with some hot 20 year old who knew how to submit to me as ruler of my house. Thank goodness King Jesus is in charge. It would have been easier but not better. I knew that I was in trouble with the Lord, because I started to have an "I don't care" attitude about what was going on with my family. I was being l-a-z-y. Then one morning He spoke to me saying, "How long are you going to tolerate this in your household?" Although Bryan was over 21 years old, according to Kingdom principles, he was still part of my household. The promise *"I'd never seen the righteous forsaken or my seed begging for bread,"* doesn't stop at 21 years old. I told the Lord, "If this is the green light, and I need to deal with it, I'll do it. You open the door to his heart, and I'll 'git-r-done'."

That afternoon, Bryan came by the store, and we went for a famous "walk with Dad." I asked him if I could see his driver's license. As I looked at it, I told him to look at his name, Bryan Charles Coker. I asked, "Did you know that you're the son of a righteous man?" He gave me one of those weird looks, which said without a word, "Yeah, Dad, I know I am." I continued on, "Bryan, do you love this girl that you're playing house with?" He said, "Yes, I do." I asked, "Do you love her enough to marry her?" He said he didn't think so. I told him that he was about to enter into a season, where he was going to reap what he'd been sowing. If he did not marry this girl, there would not be a covenant between him and her, which meant that I could not go into the courts of heaven and ask for her to be born-again. I gave him very clear instructions, "You either marry her, or I'm going to start praying against her. You may have to bury her. She is demonic and is trying to destroy you and our family. I will not tolerate it any longer."

Bryan was offended and angry with me. He called his older brother, the theologian, to tattle on me and got his mother all riled up. That made me even more determined to drive that woman out of his life. She could go standing up or lying down in a box. Either way, she was going!!

About five weeks later, Bryan came by the house and sat down on the couch. He wondered, "Dad, does Heaven do what you ask it to do? Three days after you told me what to do and I blew you off, we got into a fight. That crazy, demon possessed, girlfriend of mine flipped out and lost her mind. I knew at that point that I had to make a decision. I knew you were praying, and this wasn't working out very well for me. I want you to know, she no longer lives with me." Boy, was Susie happy to hear that! We could see Bryan was starting to make better choices in his life, but he avoided me quite a bit. The youngest boy is always a mama's boy. (Like father, like son)

A few months later, I had a prophetic dream. In this dream, a policeman knocking on my front door, awakened me in the middle of the night. As I shook the officer's hand, I saw Bryan huddled in the corner by the door. I looked over the shoulder of the policeman, and into the neighborhood. I saw many fires all around the neighborhood, except for my property and couldn't understand why my property had been spared. The police officer said to me, "Mr. Coker, I recognize you're a man of great authority, but I have a problem with your son, Bryan. He has been convicted of a crime, and he's going to be sentenced to prison." I questioned, "Are you positive that he is guilty?" He said, "Yes, look at all those fires. He is responsible for them all over the city, and it is a crime." As I looked down at Bryan, he looked up into my eyes. I said, "Son, I've always tried to teach you, if you're going to do the crime, you have to do the time." The officer kept on, "Mr. Coker, you seemed a little distraught when I said that he had to go to the big house." I spoke quietly, "Yes, in order to survive the big house, Bryan will have to harden his heart. If he hardens his heart in prison, he will not be able to hear God's voice, and therefore be unable to fulfill his dreams." The policeman said, "Mr. Coker, I am a man of authority myself. I recognize that you also have tremendous authority, and I acknowledge from where you get your authority. Sir, I'll tell you what I can do. I have a friend who has a work camp. If I send Bryan to the work camp, he'll have supervision, and oversight. He will be taught discipline, so he will not have to harden his heart. He'll still be able to hear God's voice and fulfill his dreams." I asked, "Would that fulfill the requirement of the judgment of his crime?" He said, "Yes." I inquired further, "Would he come out from the work camp with a clean slate and no record?" He said, "Yes, sir." I said, "Sir, if you could do that, I would greatly appreciate it." He shook my hand. When I woke up from this dream, my first question was, "What in the hell has this boy gotten himself into now?"

The following day Bryan came by the office to get a check from his mommy, because he had a dentist appointment. (I still don't know why we were paying his dentist bill.) I sat down and told Bryan about the dream that I had. As I was talking, Bryan said, "Dad, I know God speaks to you. I will take that as a warning." I said, "Bryan, I don't think you understand. It's not a warning. Judgment has already been executed. I am a righteous father, and I have tremendous authority. After this dream last night, I went to the courts of heaven, and negotiated the boundaries of your judgment. It's up to you to make the corrections in your life." That stern father look came upon my face. I bellowed, "You had better straighten up and fly right. Do you hear me!?!"

Several months later, Susie came to me. She felt like it was time for Bryan to move back home. I made the bold statement, "absolutely not."

We had peace in our home, and I enjoyed not having my children living with me. (I was going to build a 1-bedroom house just so they couldn't come back.) I could tell Susie wasn't happy with my answer, but I wasn't changing my mind. She waited a few weeks. One day she sat down with me and said, "Listen, I have something I want to talk over with you. I don't want you to give me an answer, until you pray about it." I said, "What is it?" She said that she felt like it was time for Bryan to come back home. She said, "He's making some choices and changes, and I believe he needs to get out of some situations. What do you think?" I reminded her, "You told me to pray about it!"

A few nights later, we went to a house church meeting that was being held in our neighborhood. During worship the Holy Spirit started speaking to me, "It is a privilege for a son to want to come back to his father's house. Bryan has made some good choices. He is now becoming teachable. Let him move back home and bless him." I was sitting over in the corner, bawling like a big baby, tears running down my cheeks. Susie came and sat next to me. I told her what the Lord said about Bryan.

Bryan coming home was a great thing. He definitely had become more teachable, and was pleasant to be around...except, he didn't clean his room when he lived there the first time, and some things never change. After several months, Bryan and Jason went to Jacksonville. THEY had decided that going in the Army would be great for Bryan. I was completely out of the loop and knew nothing about it. Susie told me that he was enlisting, and he'd gone to Jacksonville to be sworn in. He got home about 1:30 in the morning. We sat on the couch, and I was curious, "Hey, I heard that you signed up for the Army." He was hesitant, "Dad, I was going to, but I realized that I did not have your blessing, so I told the recruiter that I would be back." He asked for my blessing, and I gave it freely and lovingly. The Army was the work camp where Bryan would find discipline and training, and still be able to hear God's voice.

The following week, Susie and I went to Jacksonville with Bryan and spent the night there. Bryan got up at four in the morning, met his recruiter, and prepared to be sworn in. After he left the hotel room, I fell back asleep, and I had another prophetic dream about him. In the dream, we were in a 747 airplane. As the plane was descending to land, I recognized that it was going to crash. Bryan was panicking, looking out the window. Everybody was terrified and screaming. Bryan looked at me and begged, "Dad, do something!" I unclipped my seat belt, stood up, pointed toward the cockpit, and yelled, "You'd better straighten up and fly right!" After I told the plane to straighten up and fly right, the pilot gained enough control to land in an open field next to a baseball diamond. The plane skidded to a stop with the nose of the plane up against the backstop fence. A sign there read, "Field of Dreams." The passengers started bailing out of all the emergency exits. We were all milling around in a state of awe because we were all safe. One FAA investigator was talking to the pilots and asking what had happened. The pilots were reporting that they knew the plane had been completely out of control. At the last moment they gained enough response of the controls to do an emergency landing. They couldn't explain it! Bryan told the investigator, "I can tell you what happened. My father told this plane to 'straighten up and fly right'." The Lord gave me a word for Bryan before he left for Iraq. It was very difficult for me to give him. I let him know that when he came home, either he would have a tender heart and the ability to hear God's voice, or he would come home in a box. The choice was his.

I can remember the first phone call home from Iraq. "Dad, did you know that when the mortars are coming in over your head, that they actually whistle? I thought that was just something that happened in the movies. They actually whistle." "So, what do you do when you hear them?" I asked. He said, "I pull the covers over my head, pretend I'm in the fort, and I feel protected like I used to at grandma's house."

Bryan had known Lori from school and church. They began to get serious when he came home on his first leave from Iraq. So, when he called me from Iraq a year later and asked permission to marry her, I wasn't surprised. He was going to make sure they had my blessing, as he didn't want me to do what I had done to his last girlfriend! They became officially engaged when Bryan came home, and we had a party at the house of Lori's parents. My whole family was there. Friends and family of Lori's mom and dad were there. We had banners that said, "Welcome home!" on one side, and "Congratulations!" on the other. Bryan had given his mother money to buy a diamond ring while he was in Iraq. (He should have known better. She spent $1500 over his budget.) As we were all toasting Bryan and Lori, and their engagement, her father took the microphone and said, "The Lord works in mysterious ways." Since her parents weren't church going people, he stunned us all. He went on to share that 13 years earlier, he and his wife Diane, were on the verge of a divorce. She had convinced him to go to a Valentine's banquet. There he heard a testimony about a man and woman whose marriage had been healed by God. He related that the impact of that testimony was so great, that he and Diane are still married today. That banquet was one of the first times Susie and I had publicly shared our testimony. We had no idea of its effects. Susie and I had a very bad fight over that speaking engagement because I felt that God told me to speak, but I didn't ask Susie before I confirmed. I got bold with her and told her I would stand in front of all those people and say God had healed our marriage. I would also say her fear had gripped her so tight that she had threatened to walk out on our marriage again. It only took Susie 13 years to understand that I had heard God, and she still hasn't admitted I was right. God has a plan!

My son, Bryan, spent five years in the Army. It was absolutely the best training of his life. Bryan came home from Iraq a man. He showed wisdom in the service and saved his combat pay. He bought a new car, purchased a house, and now has a precious baby girl (my cute granddaughter). He has finished his training to become a police officer and is now enrolled in college, finishing a degree in criminal justice. He is absolutely successful and never should be begging for bread.

A few days after the prophetic dream that I had about Bryan and the airplane, I had another encounter with God. This was different than a prophetic dream. I was literally taken out of my body and seated in a courtroom setting. It wasn't a large public courtroom, but it was more of a council chamber. Those who were in the room had the spiritual responsibility for the city of Hornell, New York, as I do. Jesus was sitting at the head of the table with two others on each side. The Lord asked me a very simple question. He asked me, referring to the pastor in New York who had murdered my character and refused to forgive me for years, "Do you believe he has lost his ability to pastor the city?" I can remember deeply searching my heart to make sure that there was no criticism or judgment in me against this man. When I answered the Lord, it would be pure and upright. I confirmed to the council members in the room, "I believe this man totally loves Jesus, but his actions, lifestyle, and inability to bring correction to his marriage have left him without the influence to properly pastor this city any longer!" I just barely finished that statement, when Jesus slammed down the gavel. He said, "It is decided, this man's mantle and responsibility are removed and given to another." I knew to whom the mantle was shifting.

The process of this particular encounter caused me to ask the Lord what test I had passed that granted me access to sit in this place of authority in the courts of heaven. The Lord said, "Last week, when you properly judged your son, I knew I could trust you with a city." In the Kingdom of God, we function as sons, kings, and priests. Sonship is our access, we judge as kings, and we bring the proper sacrifices between heaven and earth to the mercy seat of God as priests.

And I bestow upon you a kingdom, just as My Father bestowed one upon Me, that you may eat and drink at My table in My kingdom, and sit on thrones judging the twelve tribes of Israel."
Luke 22:29-30

After this short season of not traveling back and forth to New York, I had been in Hornell on vacation and ran into Brother Casterline. He told me about a prophet who called him out in North Carolina. This guy was very accurate about him personally and the church of Hornell. During the conversation he said that if he had the money he would have this guy come to the church and have some regional meetings. I heard the Lord tell me to give him $1500 to help support these meetings Then the Lord had Susie and me fly up to be in the meetings. I asked God what He was up to, but all He told me was to be alert.

The night before we were to fly to New York I had a prophetic dream. In the dream I was walking down a hallway in a suit coat with several people behind me. As I walked I saw a man, dressed about the same, coming to shake my hand. As our hands touched, we turned into track stars, dressed in running clothes, and running in a relay race in a large stadium. As I turned the corner I handed him the baton. We successfully completed the hand off. As he continued running, the whole group, which had been running behind me, kept running after this guy. As I stopped in the track I realized the group was made up of the friends, leaders and people from the Hornell area that I had been ministering to for years. I stood in the middle of the track trying to catch my breath while watching them run after this guy. The Lord said, "What you have been running after is going to be handed to this prophet, because the city wants a prophet and not YOU. They can have what they want, but be on guard and protect them if you can." When we arrived in Hornell, I finally met Bob, the guy in the dream.

At the service that night my wife was late coming into the meeting with my sister Becky. I remember this part because I was a little hot since they were late. This guy was off the chain accurate, and I was very impressed with his gift.

The next morning we arranged a breakfast meeting with Bob, Susie, and me. We picked him up at his hotel. Susie was sitting in the backseat and asked Bob for a word. Susie has never been impressed with people who are prophets. She is married to one and has cleaned up behind me for years. She also has a very keen gift of discernment. She doesn't have to know what's wrong to know something is wrong. She just knows. It was very unlike her to ask for a word.

He started off, "Last night when you came into the church late, I saw you in the spirit before you closed your heart to me." He said, "You're one hard-a_ed woman. You're not very impressed with the gifts." He told her that he saw her arguing with me about her traveling in ministry when I needed her to come. That she was to be my protection from the traps of the enemy. He called out her gifting and then started to tell us that we were going to start a church. He told us we needed to have a church because it's the only way God would be able to train us. He shared that he had made some very bad mistakes in his pastoring ministry a few years earlier. He gave me an example about a prophetic couple he had. The husband was a prophet and his wife was a great prophetic worship leader from South Africa. They were one of the best he had ever been around. He told me that he made some mistakes and hurt them. He said that I needed to have some of life's lessons like that, also. He explained that was why I needed to pastor a church.

I asked later ,about this couple, a prophet and a great worship leader. I asked if he had ever repented to them and if they were healed from the wounding that he inflicted. His answer shocked me. He said, "Hell, I don't know. They left and went back to his hometown. That's not my problem anymore." So I asked where they lived, and he told me Deland, Florida. I asked their names, but the shocked look on my face was a small tip. After he found out I also live in Deland, he never did give me their names.

For two years, God had me pray for the highly gifted couple that an ignorant prophet had hurt and who was not man enough to ask their forgiveness and get them healed. As the dream showed, all of Hornell started running after this guy. He came back several times and preached in different churches. He put together a trip to Indiana with some of the leadership's kids of a church in town. God told me to make the trip and make sure that I was with the team at all times. Bob took his wife on this trip. She told me one day that she was glad I was in Bob's life and hoped he would take some of my advice. I was sent by God to protect my Hornell kids from a predator prophet. Because I didn't explain myself to the leadership in Hornell, they automatically assumed I was a best friend with this guy. This was beginning of the exposure of this prophet's sins by God to Brother Casterline and others in New York.

Bob never wanted to build relationship since I called him on the carpet on the trip to Indiana. After the years of praying for this couple Bob wounded, I was invited to a meeting in my city of Deland, where I finally met Hank and his wife. The speaker at this meeting was Louis DeSiena, a friend of Hank's, from Jacksonville. As he was speaking, the

Lord told me he was a Kingdom apostle. I was in no frame of mind to hear that. Then the Lord told me that He was going to open the door for a relationship with Louis. I had had it with self-proclaimed apostles, so I told God that if that were true, then he had to sow into my life first, before I would consider a relationship with him. Louis called me out and gave me a word from the Lord. Then he went to his book table and gave me a copy of everything he had. At one time I asked Louis to father me. Thank God for his wisdom to say no. We are brothers, and are still in relationship today.

Hank and I have been friends for years now. He used my building for a season, then opened a church in Deland called Vivid Life Church. God has a plan to expand His kingdom and it is on schedule...

Kingdom Keys:

1. When I choose the proper time, I will judge uprightly.

2. No judging until God closes the window of longsuffering.

3. A man's heart motives are more important than his gifting.

4. Taking responsibility includes protecting the innocent. It also includes good communication with those having the same responsibility.

Round 11

A Trip to China with My Dad

The lighting company, under Jason's management, was growing at a tremendous pace. We opened a distribution center in Orlando. Our corporate office was in Orange City, and we started doing business with national builders. One day, I was making a delivery to one of them in Vero Beach. The Lord spoke to me at the intersection of Kings Highway and Route 60. He said to me, "I want you to open a lighting store in Vero Beach, because I want to restore your lost inheritance." This didn't sit well with me, because this was my hometown; our family goes back five generations in this county. Plus, this was the place of my shame... The adultery that both Susie and I had committed that had threatened to tear apart our marriage had happened there... for all the town to see. Truth be known, we had recovered from that season, but I did not want to deal with the demonic warfare that had taken me out before, or face some of the people from the past. But the Lord said, "Restore my lost inheritance."

When God said He wanted to restore my lost inheritance, my carnal mind said, "I had a lot more money when I lived in Vero than I do now. Is God going to restore the finances I had lost?" Spiritual thought... "Or is it for a greater purpose?"

So I told Jason what God told me, and he started crunching the numbers. He calculated how much gas, time, and energy we would use doing business over 100 miles away from our corporate office. He projected new growth, and he put a business plan together. So, we started looking for a location. We found a great location right on US Highway 1.

We finished the construction of the showroom, and the week we opened, I got a phone call from a Christian businessman I knew in Vero Beach. He started off by asking, "Charlie, how much does that billboard cost you a month?" "What billboard?" He said, "The billboard you just had put up beside your new showroom." I said, "Brian, I haven't paid for any billboard." He said, "It has to be yours." I drove to the showroom for the first day of business in Vero Beach. I came through the back door and unlocked the front door of the showroom. I looked to the right, and there was a huge billboard painted all black with a picture of Jesus. Below the picture was the inscription, *"they will know them by their love one for another."* (John 13:35) As I looked at this billboard, the Holy Spirit spoke to me saying, "Charlie, I've given you your billboard as a display to your hometown of the grace that is on your life." To my amazement, there was no name or phone number telling who put this billboard up. So I took a picture of it and sent it to Pastor Larry. Then I called him. I reminded him about the opportunity to be a billboard of God's Grace. I had gotten my billboard. For over six months that billboard was the talk of the town. Everybody thought I was the one who put it up. For years it had been well known that my marriage had been a public display of disgrace, but I had found Christ in a powerful way. Now, the whole town knew that I was back.

God has a good sense of humor! I didn't know that I would start spending three nights a week at my Dad's house. My father was having heart issues, and he had multiple surgeries. I have a sister in New York who is a registered nurse, yet God put me in the position of caring for him. This was all part of the plan of restoring my inheritance. A new relationship at a spiritual level with my father had begun to flower.

During this season, my father and I became very close. We started dealing with some of the hurts and wounds that had occurred over the years. After all these years, I still wanted my father's approval. I had finally gotten a blessing as his son, but he was unwilling to publicly declare that he was proud of me. "When you do business with the Son, you do business with Me." I heard the Father say. The boxing match continued, because we were into two different systems—Church Fathers vs. Kingdom Sons!

For I have come to set a man against his father, a daughter against her mother, and a daughter-in-law against her mother-in-law...
Matthew 10:35

One night my father asked if I wanted to go to a special meeting that was taking place at New Hope Church, where he attended. That night the guest speaker was Jack Taylor. He preached about the "Cosmos," with a PowerPoint presentation on how big God is. The Lord showed me that this man would become my spiritual father, before God would release me into my true ministry calling. Whoopee! By this time I had been asking for over 10 years for a spiritual father. I got to where I really didn't care anymore. So I put God to the test boldly stating, "If this is true, have Jack Taylor sow into my life first, with no prompting from me."

After the meeting when we were preparing to leave, Pastor Jack Hart called me over to meet Jack. He introduced me as a great young preacher. Papa Jack was very kind and friendly. He turned to his book table and gave me a book to read, but only if I promised to read it in the next 30 days. I promised and we left. While I was in bed that night, I asked God why I had to wait for a mentor or a spiritual father. He told me it's all about His timing. I complained that Jack had written several books, but he gave me a book written by someone else. The one Jack gave me was *The Unshakable Kingdom and the Unchanging Person* by E. Stanley Jones. This guy was old when he wrote this book. How old was he? When E. Stanley Jones was born, the Dead Sea was only sick. Now that's old. It's a great book, by the way! When Papa Jack got in my car 8 years later and saw that I was reading this book, I had to admit I never did read it within the promised 30 days. Confession is always good for the soul.

My dad did admit that he kept me at arm's length much longer than he should have. He wasn't sure about my positions, and some of the challenges I exposed about the church system. He was a leader in the church system, and my gifting and overzealousness had become a threat to that. I think he was concerned about his reputation, but he asked me to forgive him for holding me at arm's length. I asked him to pray a father's blessing over me.

Needless to say, I had to pretty much walk him through it, because he had never done that before. When my grandfather died, he was almost 11 years old. But at the graveside, he was told that he was now the man of the house. He had to take care of his mother and brother. (What a load of crap to dump on an 11 year old!) That made him a natural orphan who was responsible for himself, and my emotionally challenged uncle. My father dragged those orphan tendencies, which are always performance-based to earn favor and blessing, into his spiritual walk.

In 2001, I asked the Lord to help me find the key to my father's heart. What he showed me was a man who beat my father when he was about 13 years old. This man had married my grandmother and was a drunk. He stole two shot guns that my grandfather had left to my father. When I asked him who this man was, my dad opened a blue box he kept on the refrigerator and presented me with this man's obituary. He said some choice words about him in a way that showed me some of my father's wounds had not been completely healed. These times with my dad were token signs that God was knitting our hearts together.

My father is a man of tremendous integrity. He protected that upstanding character with a vengeance. He forced his children to flee all appearances of evil, so that we would not disrespect the church, or the things of God. In my opinion, most of it was performance-based and not heart driven. When the fear of man and man's opinion molds your behavior, it can become religious activity very quickly.

One of the biggest resentments that I had against my father came because of a misunderstanding. When I was seven, the 17-year-old son of a deacon in the church sexually abused me at knifepoint. (He later died on death row for a double murder.) The deacon was a friend of my father's. I told this man what his son had done to me, and he assured me that he would talk to my father and deal with the situation. For years, I thought my father had been told what had happened. But the deacon never communicated with my dad what actually happened. So I had the false assumption that my Dad knew and never protected me. I harbored great resentment, because my whole life, I felt like I had taken one for the religious team, so it wouldn't look bad for the church. I believe some of my anger toward the church stemmed from the bitterness that I held in my heart, because of that.

The weekend in New York, when I got in trouble because I called the pastor's wife a Jezebel and the pastor an Ahab, I shared my testimony in the men's group on Saturday morning. My father was there too, and after the meeting, my dad said that he had never heard that story. But since I had carried that wound for over 30 years, I had a hard time believing that no one knew about the abuse I had suffered. As Dad and I put a timeline together, it happened about the time the church was going through a church split, and this deacon and my father were at odds, so nothing was ever said. The sense of abandonment I felt, festered, taking 30 years to heal. All the years I believed my father hadn't protected me, and that it had been covered up to protect the church's reputation, finally made sense.

My father is a man's man, and was a strong father in the culture and environment of our home. As a result of the abuse when I was seven, a homosexual spirit tried to entrap me during my teenage years. Because I had a strong father in the home, I turned to heterosexual pornography and not homosexuality. I will explain in more detail in the book "From Rape to Righteousness, Redeeming the Bride of Christ." I believe the reality of Sonship and the father's blessing can, and will, heal sexual brokenness and homosexuality. I have witnessed the power of a spiritual father praying a blessing over a son, and have seen, personally, how it brought deliverance from the tormenting homosexual spirit that the son had been battling.

I wondered to the Lord how all of this was restoring my inheritance. He showed me that when a father and son can deal with the root issues of their problems, get healed, and bless one another, the inheritance of the Kingdom manifests in a powerful way.

It was about this time that the Lord spoke to me and said, "You are in training and are learning to father your father." I can remember spending hours talking to Dad about wanting to be in fulltime ministry. He repeatedly reminded me that being in business was ministry. I was fruitful, impacted people's lives, and expanded the Kingdom. Due to his church mindset he couldn't see how I fit, or how I would ever be successful in a church setting. Let's face it; at this point I didn't have a pastoral bone in my body. Based on my history, I hadn't been accepted or successful in that system, but I knew the calling was like fire shut up in my bones.

By this time it had been 10 years since my mother had passed away. Betty, my dad's girlfriend has a son who is a missionary to China. My dad started putting a trip together with Mama Betty, and his pastor Jack Hart. The Lord asked me if I would go to China and look after my father. His health was actually in pretty good shape at this time, so I had a feeling God was up to something. As we boarded the airplane for our 18-hour flight to Hong Kong, the Holy Spirit asked me to take some time and read all of the Minor Prophets; I took out my Bible, and I started reading. At the conclusion of reading all the Minor Prophets, The Lord asked me what I saw. I said Lord, "What I see in Scripture is a divided kingdom. What I see is a Northern tribe, and a Southern tribe. Lord, what I see is two triangles. Just like America, Israel was divided."

This trip to China was exceptionally beautiful. Betty's son Pete had lived there for 20 years, so he was the best tour guide money could buy. We had a great time traveling with Pastor Jack Hart and his wife, my father and Betty, and a few other people.

Our guide Pete had lived in China for over 20 years and took us to work with some of the underground churches. We saw what he had been doing through the educational system, building relationships, and expanding the Kingdom. It was exciting to see what God was doing in this land. He then took us to an aboveground church that was several hundred people strong. To visit in this church, showing your passport was required, so the congregation was mostly missionaries and other foreigners. The morning before we went to this church service, the Lord had given me a vision about a ripped net. Because of broken relationships the fish were escaping through the holes that were in the net. As the Lord showed me this vision, I knew the net had not been repaired, but could have been. The broken relationships were due to offenses and an unwillingness to ask for forgiveness; so the great harvest was slipping away.

On the way to the church meeting, the Holy Spirit told me that He wanted me to release a word. He said, "Tell them to fix the broken relationships, or I will send some of them home. Remind them that this is not the first time I have brought this situation to the leadership." I started pleading with God, "Please don't make me do this in front of my father." I told God how much he despised it when a prophet gives a word of correction, especially me. The Lord God was stern, "Do you fear Me more than your father?" The Lord knew the answer to that, but I was trying to weasel out of it.

I made a deal with God; I would not tell anyone that I had this word, and He had to supernaturally put the microphone in my hand. While the preacher was preaching his message, he stopped in mid sentence, pointed at me and said, "Prophet, do you have a word?" I took the microphone and explained the vision I'd had that morning. In my explanation, I told them that they had broken relationships within the body there, and with other churches in the city. I told them that the Lord was bringing this out publicly, because they had refused to deal with it when it was brought to them privately.

After church, we all went to lunch. When we returned to our hotel room, as the door closed behind me, my father decided it was time to reprimand me. He asked me, "Who in the heck do you think you are?" He then challenged the word that I gave. I acted like an eight-year-old and shut down. I looked at Dad with tears in my eyes, and said, "I think you were happier with me when I was running around in the bars. You prayed for me to get saved, but I think I got saved more than you like." That day I decided to stand against the religious controlling spirit which my father had used to manipulate me my whole life. I told God my father would never again dominate and control what I did when it came to the matters of the kingdom. Several days later, Pete took us to work with some underground churches. One of the leaders was there from the church where I had released that word. He asked if he could speak with me privately. I told him it was okay to say whatever he wanted to in front of my father. He let me know that the word that I had released was very accurate, and it was not the first time they had heard it. The leadership said that they would replay the word and fix each broken relationship, as God revealed it. Then he thanked me for my boldness. My dad looked at me, "Well, I feel silly." As I looked at my father I said to him, "And the problem is, you think that's the first time."

On this particular trip I was having a hard time containing my zeal and that kind of irritated my father. He felt like I was dominating every conversation with some new fresh revelation, but that's what we do as orphans.

Kingdom Key:
It is not good to have zeal without knowledge, nor to be hasty and miss the way. Proverbs 19:2 (NIV)

I didn't know God was about to deal with the issue of unsanctified zeal within my life, but gaining an understanding of zeal without knowledge was one of the major steps in my healing.

We had a great trip in China and boarded the airplane to head back home. As I sat in the airplane seat rehearsing the events of the trip with the Lord, He asked me how I saw the condition of the church in China. I'd always heard the underground house churches of China had become the new role model of what God was doing on the earth. What I saw in the house churches in China, definitely has a place and can be effective in expanding the Kingdom. There is also a huge aboveground church in China, but the two are divided. I saw the two triangles of systems completely separate. The house church as one triangle, and the aboveground church as the other. Two triangles had not yet found the holy sweet spot where the two blended. As I pondered this, the Lord spoke to me, "I want to show you what I'm about to do on the

earth." I went into a vision. I saw the two triangles under extreme pressure get mashed together, and as the two triangles came together I saw that they formed the Star of David. In the middle of the Star of David I saw a picture of Christ. God said, "Charles, the body of Christ is leaving the church age, and I'm in the process of birthing the Kingdom. The old system still has foundational principles from which I can bring my Kingdom." He then said that the older would serve the younger.

The Lord said the church had entered into the same season as when John the Baptist started crying in the wilderness. He asked me, "Why haven't you asked Me why I had John the Baptist's head cut off?" I asked the Lord if He actually did that. I thought Satan did it. He then informed me that He was sovereign. He told me that John the Baptist was the end of the Old Testament prophets, and Jesus was the transitional prophet from the old to the new. God told me that He had John the Baptist's head cut off so that when He gave the baton to Jesus it was headless. Christ is the head of the church. He told me to warn the arrogant and prideful pastors that He's going to start coming with a sword just like He did in the days of John the Baptist, and for them to be careful and not lose their heads.

The Lord then asked me if I would go home and start a church. He said that He would give me discernment about people that I needed as a pastor. He would show me different areas in their lives where I could bring healing and insight to their destinies, which is the triangle with the point up. God would also give me discernment about the gifts I needed to move underneath and apostolically push up. This is the Kingdom triangle with the point down. He gave me the name of the church, "One Kingdom Fellowship." I told the Lord that I did not have the strengths and capabilities to do it. I complained that I did not have the grace to be a pastor. The Lord told me Greg would give me the grace to pastor, but I would be functioning as an apostle in the ministry. He'd given me Pastor Greg to co-pastor with, and that Greg would function as a prophet. We would become an apostolic and prophetic team.

We landed at Orlando International Airport after flying all day from China. We stood at the curb, hugging and kissing, getting ready to go our separate ways. I hugged my father and whispered in his ear, "Dad, if you ever again usurp the spiritual authority God has given me, the next time God asks me if it's time for you to go home to be with Him in heaven, I will tell Him, 'Yes, take him.' I love you and I respect you, but don't undermine my authority again when I'm operating in my gifting." That day the control was broken. An authority shift took place.

A couple of weeks after we were home from the China trip, I was at my dad's house. I couldn't sleep, so rather than toss and turn, I got up at 1:30 a.m. and drove home. Halfway home in the pitch dark on I-95, I started weeping and crying. I asked the Lord what sin I had committed that made me lose my zeal for Him. The Lord asked me why I thought I had sinned. "Holy Spirit, it must be a sin that would make me lose my zeal for you," I cried. The Lord spoke to me and said, "No, Son, I took your zeal for Me away!" I then asked, "Why in the world would You take it away?" He continued, "I have been trying to take you to a place of maturity. I had to remove your zeal for Me to make room to deposit the zeal of Me."

This was the beginning of my path to Sonship. Sonship learns to lean back and work **from** inheritance, instead of working **for** your inheritance. When you're an orphan, you use your energy and zeal for Him in the hopes that you're pleasing to God. Sonship has the zeal of Him, and true relationship as a son, therefore you do the father's business with His blessing. This does not require nearly the same amount of energy.

It was about this time that the Lord gave me a vision of a triangle that covered Florida. It started north of Jacksonville, proceeded down the east coast to about Stuart, went west over to the Tampa area, and back up to north Florida. Right in the middle of the triangle is where I live in Central Florida. I started a campaign just like I had done in New York, and I have driven every town and every village in that triangle. As I traveled, I repented for the sins of the church and of the leadership. I asked God to send revival. It was obvious He was giving me responsibility in the area of the triangle, and wherever He would send me, I would have authority in the spiritual realm. Please don't think that I think that I'm all that and a bag of chips. I know that I'm only one of perhaps hundreds of people God has called within this triangle to do their part. But where the King is giving us responsibility, the Kingdom is starting to expand within those borders of that authority.

Kingdom Keys:

1. *It is not good to have zeal without knowledge, nor to be hasty and miss the way.* Proverbs 19:2 (NIV)

2. Maturity means being transformed from having zeal **for** God to having the zeal **of** God.

3. Wisdom is knowing when and how to use the knowledge we have been given.

Round 12

Birthing the Church

For many years Pastor Greg and I had talked about starting a church together. He'd been one of the pastors at Trinity, then the associate pastor under Pastor Larry. After he'd been in that position a few years, the Lord gave me a revelation that the ministry was taking a toll on Greg's marriage. The Lord asked me to give Greg a job at my lighting store. I told the Lord I didn't have a position for him at that time, but was willing to do whatever He told me to do. Greg and I went to a prophetic training school at Bishop Bill Hammond's in north Florida. While we were riding back, I shared the revelation with him that God had given me. The Lord had told me that if I didn't get him out of the ministry, his marriage would be in trouble. So, we made the decision that he would come to work for me. The week we were gone, my warehouse manager turned into Mr. Stupid, and cussed out one of my best customers. He was fired, so Greg took his place the following week.

Greg had become my best friend and spiritual confidant. He was also my pastor, to whom I submitted. Now, I was his boss, and he had to submit to me. Add my oldest son Jason into the mix, and we were both submitting to a younger man at work. It was an unusual arrangement because Jason submitted to the both of us at church.

Kingdom key:
When the foundation of Love supports the archway of Honor, then the door of God's favor opens to you!

When there are multiple arenas of authority, you have to be careful not to cross those lines. When you do, you need to address them and fix them. Most people want authority, but few take responsibility for that authority.

Kingdom key:
You only have authority in the areas where you have taken responsibility.

You can find a person's realm of authority by looking at what responsibility they've taken upon themselves. Too many church people want a title to give them authority, but have never taken the responsibility in the realm of the spirit or the natural. Pastor Greg and I experienced this years ago when we were doing the house church and deliverance ministry. I continued to submit to him, because he had been my spiritual authority, instead of taking my rightful place and leading. One time when a crisis manifested, checks had to be written, responsibility taken, and hard decisions made. It fell on me. Greg checked out and vanished for three days. He left me to make the hard decisions. I made them because I was responsible for the outcome, which resulted in an authority shift in our relationship.

Kingdom key:
During an authority shift, there is at least a three day death and resurrection process. If you allow this three day disconnect to be Holy Spirit led, you can reconnect properly aligned.

If the body of Christ would actually learn this principle, people would not split churches to become promoted in the Kingdom.

I went on a 40 day water only fast. During this time, the Lord started debating with me about starting the church. We argued for 39 days. You can only argue with God so long before He pulls His God card and tells you, "You will obey me." For some reason, He thinks He's God! I explained to the Lord that my company was attached to the building trade in Florida, and it was heading into the economic toilet very quickly. There was absolutely no way I could financially support a church!

I know every good pastor starts in faith and obedience, but I was not one of them. I was a strong-willed, opinionated orphan, who loved God with all my heart, but fought God every step of the way. I decided to negotiate with God, and see if He was serious about this church stuff. I told Him that because the church had been financially raped, I was not going to stand in a pulpit every Sunday and beg for tithes and offerings. I told Him if He was serious, He had to give me the money up front, so all the bills would be paid for at least two years. None of this blind faith stuff. If He did that, I would know He was serious.

I finished the 40 day fast. Afterward, I sat down with Jason and Susie and told them what the Lord had said. Immediately both of them responded with record-breaking negativity. "Dad, we're struggling in the business." "Charlie, you don't have one pastoral bone in your body. You don't even like churches." While all that was true, I told them that I had made a deal with God. If He would pay for it up front, then I would do it. "What are the chances of God doing that?" I thought God would bail on the whole thing.

There was a businessman who owned a shopping center in Deltona. In the corner of that shopping center, Mark and Phyllis Gregory had a church for over five years. At one time, I had actually gone to that church and been part of their fellowship. For nine years, Phyllis had run a community outreach center from that space. The businessman decided to sell the shopping center, but the purchaser wanted the space to have a three-year tenant. Phyllis had been offered another building by the city and planned to move. I learned all this information later. The businessman told me he felt that I was to have a church in that building and gave me over $225,000 to pay the rent. Yeah, that was a "Jehovah Sneaky." To my surprise, God was actually serious about me starting a church, but my heart and passion were to travel. I had been functioning in the triangle of authority in New York on and off for 16 years. Now, God was showing me a triangle of authority in Florida. But, pastoring?!? Me?!? Lord, you've got be kidding!

The Lord was bringing revelation about starting the church. He had shown me that the government structure always comes in threes, Father, Son, and Holy Spirit; Abraham, Isaac, and Jacob; and even Apostle, Prophet, and Teacher.

Kingdom key:
Anytime you find government you will find three elements within the principle.

God was designing and facilitating this church thing. I started asking the Lord how it was going to work with Greg and me. Greg is the most loving, kind pastor you've ever met in your life. I'm a raw prophet, trying to go through the death process of becoming an apostle. God's been trying to restore me and take away my orphan thinking and insecurities. I believed that if I didn't have Greg with me, I would be weak and ineffective as a leader, just like I felt I needed a partner at the store. Greg's strength was pastoral, and I knew I needed that.

I went into a vision. The Lord revealed that when Greg was young, he had a prophetic word given to him that went something like this, "You will function as a pastor, but in your latter years you will operate as a prophet." I brought this revelation to Greg. He totally confirmed that it was from God, because he had not shared that with anyone. In this model, I was to function as an apostle, Greg was to function as a prophet, with my son Jason serving as the teacher. This structure worked.

> *And in the church God has appointed first of all apostles, second prophets, third teachers, then workers of miracles, also those having gifts of healing, those able to help others, those with gifts of administration, and those speaking in different kinds of tongues. 1 Corinthians 12:28 (NIV)*

During the time God was preparing me to start a church, I had credentials with an apostolic network. I called my overseer, looking for some counsel on how to pioneer a church. After about eight or nine phone calls, I realized I was either being ignored or God was shutting that door. Since I believe in authority, I believe in submitting to authority. I was getting mixed signals from those I was connected with. I prayed and asked the Lord what was going on. He asked me what the official start date for the lease was. I told Him January 1, 2008. He inquired, "When do your credentials need to be renewed?" I pulled out my credentials card and saw that the renewal date was January 1, 2008. The Lord then said to me, "This is a new season of your life, and I'm going to bring men into your life who will be counsel to you, father you, and teach you the things that you do not know."

I no longer had a spiritual authority to submit to, a totally new concept for me. In some ways it was quite scary. If you are burdened by true insecurities, and still think like an orphan, there are many pitfalls that can be avoided by listening to those who have been down the same road before you. The Lord told me that the blueprint for me to build on was already inside of me. I would need to walk it out day by day.

Greg and I decided that the genuine structure would be the apostle/prophet positioning between us, but publicly we would co-pastor as equals. I had no problem with that, because I was totally secure in his ability to hear God and to make decisions. We had learned to trust one another over the previous 18 years both as co-workers and friends. Many doubters believed that there couldn't be two heads, and this would never work. Privately, Greg and I never made a decision that we did not agree on. That was a great safety net for me as it helped cover my insecurities and fears.

Greg had a tremendous seer gift. He saw angels and all kinds of things in the spirit realm. He was great at the prophetic, and all those years that he served as a pastor made us a great team. He had been on dozens of missionary trips to Russia and all over Europe. He'd been to South America and the Dominican Republic numerous times. Greg even took a year off while he worked at the store to become a missionary trainer in the Bahamas. He would light up like a Christmas tree on the mission field. He took some of our leaders on a mission trip to Honduras. They saw thousands of people saved, blind eyes opened, deaf ears healed, and even a dead baby came back to life.

We adopted the logo of the two triangles coming together in forming One Kingdom. That's how we structured our leadership. The first few years were an absolute joy. During that time, I traveled to New York and Pennsylvania. While I was gone, Greg was at the church preaching and pastoring, the perfect fit.

Pastoring week to week was much more difficult than I ever imagined. Trying to pastor people who were hurt and wounded was starting to take a toll on me. One day in prayer, I asked the Lord to help me to become a better pastor, and His answer shocked me. The Lord let me know that He couldn't help in that department because of my own words. I went to a vision and overheard myself speaking, "I'm not a pastor, I will never pastor, and I don't even like most pastors." The Lord said to me, "You made a vow that I cannot break. Until you break the vow, I cannot release the pastoral grace and anointing that you need to minister to my people." So I started asking for forgiveness and breaking the vow.

Kingdom Key:
Don't make stupid vows you have to renounce later.

It was amazing! I even started liking the children. The Lord reminded me of an incident when I was in Pastor John's church. I was walking through the kitchen, and there were two young boys who were absolute hoodlums in our church. Pastor John was on the floor wrestling with both of them, and as I walked by, one boy said, "Pastor John, Pastor John. See that man right there? He doesn't play." Even though that was true, it broke me to repentance.

Our church attracted several strong women who were very gifted and others who were very wounded. When I look back at this, I see that it was God sending people that the church system had rejected. These were women with control issues, hurt by husbands or religion, but God was changing my heart and had given me the insight to their destinies. I became very patient compared to how I used to be. To my own detriment, I started to tolerate things in people that I shouldn't have, but I could see the individual's God-given callings. God was starting to break my heart and give me a love that I previously did not have. Many years ago, God gave me a vision of a large army of women ushering in a great harvest of souls. This helped me understand why I was leading all these gifted women.

I would have to say at least 75% of the time, Greg and I would come to church, compare notes, then tag preach. By honoring each other's gifts and talents, we were demonstrating the Kingdom at a level that many had never seen. We are all interdependent on each other. This is shown as we appreciate each other's uniqueness and learn to depend on each other. When Greg and I started the church, we knew the key would be worship, so we started praying for a worship leader sent by God. At one point, we got desperate enough that we tried to hire a guy from Alabama. That didn't work. In my frustration, I started praying one day about it. The Lord broke into my prayers and said, "The problem is you want your version of a worship team, not the one that I want." I asked Him, "What do You want for a worship team?" As is my pattern, I went into a vision where there were nine warehouses. The ninth warehouse garage door was open, and inside was a heavy metal band. They were playing the most god-awful, growling, loud music I'd ever heard. I despised it. As I was walking up to the band, the guys asked, "Can we help you?" I said, "Yes, I am Pastor Charlie Coker from One Kingdom Fellowship. I want you guys to come on Sunday and lead worship at my church." They all started laughing and said they were not Christians. "I will take care of that in a minute, but on Sunday I want you to come and do worship." They were smoking and drinking, and had tattoos all over their bodies. I led them to the Lord in the vision and they became my worship team.

I couldn't believe this was God's choice! It totally exposed my religious judgments and criticisms. I released this word for six or eight weeks to the church. Then one Sunday morning, I looked at the second row. The Lord reminded me what they looked like. I started picking them out. "You're the lead singer with flames on your guitar, you're the bass player, and you're the drummer. I led them all to the Lord that day. Monday night they came to practice, and were completely surprised that they could play normal music. Pastor Greg was actually there with them. Everyone was shocked at the anointing that showed up in the room. The name of their band was "Hog Breeders." They changed the name to "Thorns of the Crown." They practiced on Thursday night, and by Sunday morning they were our worship team.

Some of my leaders and I went to a place called the "Dungeon." We were amazed how those in the heavy metal culture honored each other and waited for each other to play and interact. I saw more Kingdom in that culture than I had seen in the church. It was because of the success of "Thorns of the Crown," that the manager of the Dungeon started having Christian heavy metal band nights once a quarter. We had Christian heavy metal bands come to the church for concerts. My father came to the church when we were having one. I figured he would absolutely lose it, but he didn't. He only made one small suggestion. He said, "Son, if I was you, I would put the words of the songs on the overhead, so that people could read the words and know they're talking about God. Otherwise, they will think it is demonic."

Our children's department began to grow and soon we were in need of a children's pastor. About this time, Greg's wife came into the church on a Sunday morning and said she had a warning dream with me in it. She said in the dream I had made Greg the children's pastor, that I had taken the lead role, and demoted Greg to be my associate. She told me that was never going to happen! "We are co-pastors," she defiantly declared! You see they had done children's ministry before, and vowed to never to do it again.

Pastor Greg and his wife became offended with some of the decisions I was making, and I don't think we ever recovered from that very first offense. The problem was, Greg was my best friend. I loved him dearly, and I truly did not know what to do. Any decisions I made were going to hurt our relationship, but because of my insecurities, I believed I would not be successful without him. The boxing match between church fathers and Kingdom sons was starting to happen between us. I knew it was happening between my father and me, and I had even experienced it between Jason and me. What I didn't realize until later, was that it was happening between Greg and me. I was starting to grow up and take my rightful position privately, which I've always done. Now, I was doing it publicly, and this is where the fight always begins. I know this is not a Bible scripture but you've heard the phrase, "all good things must come to an end."

I started taking trips, focusing my efforts and attention on New York and Pennsylvania, and that started to take its toll on One Kingdom Fellowship. I still can't get the promise from God out of my head, concerning the vision He gave me in 1996 about a move of God that becomes a revival. This vision included the Glory Cloud of God showing up, and people instantly converted to the King of Kings and Lord of Lords. I didn't want to go back to the area any longer and start my own man-made revival. I wanted the real deal. Lord knows, I didn't want another fake Rolex.

The Lord was speaking to me about going back to New York when an invitation came with a specific date. As I pondered this request to go preach, I asked the Lord if this was still practice, or if this was the real season, and the right timing for the release of the Kingdom. He assured me this was no longer practice. I had entered into the season of no return. Being bold I said to Him, "You promised me a Harley, and a Rolex on that mountaintop in 1996 as a sign of the coming season of revival. When you give me the Harley, then I'll go back to New York and preach!"

Several days later, my wife asked if I had bought my airplane tickets for New York, and I informed her that I decided I would not go to New York until I got my Harley Davidson motorcycle. She stated, "I know what you're going to do. You'll wait until the last minute. God will speak to you, and then you will pay 3 times what you should for your airplane ticket." I said, "No, if I don't get my Harley I'm not going. I preach every Sunday. I don't need a place to preach anymore, and I don't need any more practice. If God is not going to do His part, I'm no longer doing mine."

About three days later, Randy, a friend of mine who owned a beautiful Harley called me up and said, "Charlie, I'm going to China to be a missionary and will be gone at least two years." The worst thing you can do to a Harley is let it sit and not use it. He brought me his Harley and the title, and said we'd figure out what to do when he got back. Well, armed with my new Harley, I bought my airplane ticket and started returning to New York on a more regular basis.

It was time to start making some decisions about the business. The economy was not doing well; my oldest son's marriage was coming apart, and my daughter-in-law was planning to move to Miami with my grandson. From July to December, I traveled through New York and Pennsylvania doing more ministry there than I did at home. Susie and I decided to go to New York for our Christmas vacation. Christmas Eve day, before we got on the airplane, a Christian businessman friend called me and wanted to have a cup of coffee. During our conversation he said that he had an encounter with the Lord about me. The Lord had shown him who I was, and that I carried a "Sons of Issachar anointing," since I understood the times and the seasons like they had. He also said that the Lord told him to give me a special Christmas present which I was not to open until Christmas day.

Before we went on vacation, I had told Susie that we had to make some major decisions about staying in business. My son Jason was definitely going to move to Miami, the economy was in shambles, and this burning desire for full-time ministry was consuming me. The Lord told me that He would take care of us. He could give me an employee to replace Jason, or we could close the business with bankruptcy, trust God and do ministry full-time. I told Susie that she needed to make the decision. Whatever I did, I was not going to bring her kicking and screaming into full-time ministry.

We decided to open the Christmas present instead of putting it in our luggage. To our surprise when we opened up the little box, there sat my blue-faced Submariner Rolex. I now had the Harley and the Rolex. God was saying, "This is the season to trust Me."

Closing the business was one of the hardest things I've ever had to do. I made things happen because of the business. I wrote my own checks, and I set my own schedule. I believe in some ways it had become my identity. God was about to change all of those things.

Kingdom Keys:

1. When the foundation of Love supports the archway of Honor, then the door of God's favor opens to you!

2. During an authority shift, there is a three-day death and resurrection process. If you allow this three-day disconnect to be Holy Spirit led, you will reconnect being properly aligned.

3. Anytime you find government, you will find three elements within the principle.

4. Don't make stupid vows you have to renounce later.

5. Kingdom name of God: "Jehovah Sneaky"

6. You only have authority in the areas where you have taken responsibility.

Sonship Authority

Round 13

You Don't Know Jack, Until You Know Jack

After getting the Harley and the Rolex, which were signs from God that Susie and I were coming into a new season of ministry, I spent more time in New York ministering in the triangle of authority from Buffalo to Syracuse and down to Hornell. I felt like the apostle Paul on my third missionary trip. The first time I functioned within the church system. The second time I was in an apostolic prophetic house church movement. This time I believed I was coming with a fresh blueprint of Kingdom principles. Moses received his pattern (blueprint) after being on the mountain of God.

And see to it that you make them according to the pattern which was shown you on the mountain. Exodus 25:40

For each of us to have the right blueprint we must get it from the same mountain of God that Moses did. What I came to realize was that I'd been missing some of the main elements of the blueprint that I was carrying.

I decided to take an extended road trip and go to a conference in Erie Pennsylvania, where Leif Hetland was speaking. After one of my friends in New York told me about this conference, the Lord spoke to me and told me to go. I had scheduled a meeting with a bishop from Buffalo who was in town, so my leaving town was pushed back to later Thursday morning. I decided to go to the meeting and then just drive all night to get to Pennsylvania for the conference.

At this breakfast meeting, I shared with the bishop my insight on the next move of God, which I believed would come out of Buffalo. I explained that when I was in Africa with Kingsley Fletcher, I had a vision that America was about to have a move of God's Spirit, not because of repentance, but because it was His timing. Studying the Charlie Finney revival shows it started in Rochester, New York. I learned it spread from Buffalo, east to Syracuse, and then south to Hornell, New York.

That particular revival should have spread to the whole nation, but it stopped 50 miles southeast of Rochester and had very little effect from there. While in Africa, God showed me a vision of the leadership of that revival, which hadn't dealt with racial issues and divisions in the church. Their sin stopped this move of God from going national. The Lord told me the sins of the father affect the third and the fourth generation. The fruit of that leadership group was now gone.

Since the influences of the previous generations had died, America was about to see a fresh move of the Spirit. I asked the Lord, "Why Buffalo?" I further learned it was one of the cities instrumental in ending slavery over 160 years ago. He showed me that Buffalo was the final gateway of the Underground Railroad for African slaves to escape America and find freedom. God said, "The gateway that the African slaves used to find freedom, will be the gateway He uses to bring true freedom back to America." After this encounter alongside a cannon in the courtyard of the Elmina Slave castle in Ghana, I came home and preached that America should prepare for black leadership. I thought it would be in the church, and I was very involved with the Promise Keeper's movement to bring reconciliation to the church and the country.

When Barack Obama became my president, I was puzzled because I didn't understand that this was a national word and not limited to the church. The first foreign trip he took was to the slave castles in Ghana. I have a picture of Anderson Cooper doing an interview with him, standing next to the same cannon in the courtyard of the Elmina Slave Castle, where I had stood. This trip to Ghana was life changing for me. God showed me the spiritual roots of racism. I was given a statement from the Lord about black leadership coming into power, "Because of the cross of Jesus Christ, there is no greater sin than to commit the sin that was committed against you." I have been pushing to empower black leadership for over 18 years within the churches in the cities where I had influence.

I explained this to the Bishop, and he got a little excited, since he owned the very property in the inner city of Buffalo that was the end of the Underground Railroad.

This is a little premature in this timeline, but let me add it anyway. Toward the end of Barack Obama's first term, I had a vision in which the Lord took me to stand in front of the statue of Abraham Lincoln in Washington. As I looked at the statue, the Holy Spirit said, "The assignment I gave Abraham Lincoln for this nation is about to come to an end. And then I'm going to turn this nation upside down with my Glory." The Lord showed me that the division of our nation is a mirror image of the division of His church. I believe God holds the leadership of His church responsible for the condition of this nation. The spirit of entitlement, that has entrenched the core belief systems of America, came into power because the church has been unwilling to deal with the entitlement mentality within its own walls. As a result a national orphan spirit was released by the church.

Needless to say after meeting with the Bishop, I was definitely itching to get on the road. I love being on the road; I seem to have some of my greatest encounters with the Lord on these trips. I was scheduled to be gone 21 days.

While I was driving in the dark mountains of West Virginia, about midnight that night, Jesus manifested and sat in the seat behind me. He started talking to me about some things going on in my life. When I asked Him why He didn't sit in the front seat, He laughed. "Where would I sit?" That's an inside private joke between us. You see, years ago, I was praying and asked Jesus to manifest, sit down in my car seat, and talk to me like a man. He told me that I didn't have room for Him, because I had three Bibles and six teaching tapes all about Him. I had made no room for Him to sit and talk, because I was too busy trying to learn about Him instead of learning from Him. I said, "Lord, I can make room very quickly." He said, "No, I'll sit right here so I can talk into your ear." As we were talking about the season that I was emerging from, He asked me if I liked the Rolex watch He had given me. "Of course I like this watch. It's a blue-faced Submariner, worth about $10,000. It's what I had always wanted. I could've bought one for myself, but You had made a promise to give it to me as a sign. Plus, it's from You," I gratefully replied. He said, "I'm glad you like it." (My first thought was, "Oh crap, He's going to ask me to give it away.") He went on, "But when you go to this conference tomorrow, you will find a man with the identical watch on his wrist. When you find him, give him your business card, and tell him to have Jack Taylor call you. It's time to get into relationship with the man that I promised you seven years ago. I promised he would father you before you entered into the ministry that I have called you to."

I arrived in Erie, Pennsylvania, only a few hours before the meetings began. The conference speaker for the first night was Leif Hetland. As he went to minister, he stretched his arms telling a story about how he had just spent two weeks in Florida with his spiritual father, Jack Taylor. Imagine my reaction when a blue-faced Submariner Rolex popped out from his sleeve! Sometimes you wonder if people think you're crazy for doing what God tells you to do. I wasn't sure about all the Sonship stuff, but I was sure that God had put this together. I needed to know that, because I am probably one of the worst skeptics you've ever met in your life, especially when I get around different ministries and all their gimmicks. I can tell you Jack Taylor is no ministry gimmick, he's the real deal. He has the integrity of my father, the intelligence of my oldest son, the swagger of John Wayne, and the love of God the Father.

I didn't understand this spiritual fathering thing. I didn't know how often I could call, I didn't know when I could call, I didn't know if I only brought praise reports, or real-life struggles. Jack told me that I could have all of him that I wanted, but I didn't know what that meant. (He has never told anyone else that since.) We started building a relationship over the cell phone at first.

I continued on my trip and arrived at my sister's house in New York, on Monday afternoon August 17, 2010. I slept a while, got up, and started reading a book about Ivan Q. Spencer. He is one of the fathers of our faith. He founded a Bible school in upstate New York, which has since trained pastors and thousands of missionaries all over the world. From the 1930s until the 1950s, he had a Bible school in Hornell and the school moved up to Lima near Rochester after his son took over. That night as I read the autobiography of Ivan Q. Spencer, the Lord spoke to me, "You know I work in 40 year cycles. Would you like a piece of the mantle that Ivan Q. Spencer carried while on earth?" "Absolutely!" I beamed! "He is one of the fathers of the faithful, a true hero in my book," I told God like He didn't know already. At that moment, a huge angel appeared in the room, and the whole atmosphere became electric. I heard the voice of my King, "Turn to the next page and receive what I have for you." On the next page was written, "August 17, 1970 Ivan Q. Spencer died," exactly 40 years to the day that I was reading it in that book.

I believe many mantles of church fathers have not been picked up, and are available for those who are hungry, thirsty, and willing to pay the price for them. You can ask God to give you what you need to be successful in the areas where you've asked for responsibility, in order to expand the kingdom.

Kingdom Key:
You can't have what you don't honor.

That weekend I preached for Dr. Phil Casterline at Living Waters Church in Hornell. Sunday was a good meeting. On Monday morning, I was headed to his office to talk to him and his wife. As I pulled into the parking lot, Papa Jack Taylor called me and said it was time for me to receive a father's blessing. He proceeded to pray and pronounce a blessing over my life. Now I'm accustomed to the anointing, but this time I felt warmth come from the inside all the way out to my finger tips. The big difference about this anointing is that it has never left. It is the anointing of Sonship. It came from the inside, and became a new normal. Some of my insecurities vanished that day. There was a completely new normal; I can still feel it in my hands today.

As I met with Brother Casterline, we began to discuss one of his children who had made some bad choices, including fathering a child out of wedlock. He was disgusted and used words that cursed his son. So I challenged him and said, "Listen, I have two sons, and they don't always do what's right, but I don't curse them." He started to get upset with me, was quoting scriptures and telling me what the Bible says with all that religious junk. Raising my voice, I yelled at him, pointed my finger directly at him and said, "He only reproduced what you are." To my surprise, he said, "How did you know I was a bastard?" I said, "I didn't, but that sure does explain a lot." We had a time of repentance and deliverance, and broke some of those things off his life. Brother Casterline is now in his mid 60s with a PhD, has been in ministry for over 40 years and has literally put hundreds of people into ministry through training schools, all while carrying this lifelong curse. As my relationship with Brother Casterline has developed, I have seen his heart and know he would never intentionally curse his son. As many of us have done in ignorance, we give a religious response, making the problem worse and not better. The blessing is greater than the curse.

The "bastard curse" affects so many people that I want to address it now. Take a look at Malachi chapter 4: 4-6 (NIV):

> *Remember the law of my servant Moses, the decrees and laws I gave him at Horeb for all Israel. See, I will send you the prophet Elijah before that great and dreadful day of the Lord comes. He will turn the hearts of the fathers to their children, and the hearts of the children to their fathers; or else I will come and strike the land with a curse.*

These are the last few verses of the Old Testament. God promised that He would send the prophet Elijah. With the anointing of a prophet, He would turn the hearts of the fathers to the children, and turn the hearts of the children to the fathers. This is the antidote needed to remove a curse from the land. You ask, "What kind of curse?" I believe He is talking about the bastard curse specifically. There was no voice from heaven between the Old Testament, and the New Testament. The time between the two testaments was 400 years. Since 40 years is a generation, it means the 10 generations imposed by a bastard curse is fulfilled. Israel had rejected God as their Father and wanted Kings like the other nations. The corrupt condition of the family and land was the byproduct of this curse.

> *A bastard shall not enter into the congregation of the Lord; even to his tenth generation shall he not enter into the congregation of the Lord. Deuteronomy 23:2 (KJV)*

If you are conceived outside of a marriage covenant, you can't find your true spiritual inheritance. That's why the marriage covenant between you and Jesus in the born-again experience is the only way to the Father. When the New Testament begins 400 years later, we read the story about God the Father's only begotten Son, Jesus. So, the first voice from heaven in over 400 years is from God. He re-engages with mankind speaking in the language of the Son. I believe the Sonship message and the father/son paradigm will bring the American Church back to wholeness as a family. As a family, we'll remove the curse off our land.

Looking at America today, we have a fatherless generation with many being conceived outside of a marriage covenant in the natural. We can set this generation free from the curse and bring restoration by getting the children to forgive and bless those very fathers who facilitated the curse. This will be the first generation that will have a legal right to a double portion inheritance.

Martin Luther had brought his own fight to the Roman Catholic Church and approximately 400 years later, Father visited us again at Azusa Street in 1906. At Azusa Street, the Shekinah Glory cloud of God was so thick that the children would play hide-and-seek in the Glory. Now, that's the children's program I want in my church! William J. Seymour, the leader of the Azusa Street Revival, gave a prophecy that stated that 100 years from then, there would be a move of the Glory one more time. It's time for the Father to visit again and heal His church. In the last 100 years there has been the restoration of the fivefold ministry gifts of apostle, prophet, evangelist, teacher and pastor. Now is the time for another visit from Father God to release the message of Sonship!

I gave an altar call at my church one Sunday, to deal directly with the bastard curse. I asked only those who had been conceived outside of a marriage covenant, abandoned, or orphaned to come forward. After we applied the blood for forgiveness, I started to have them follow me in a prayer. I asked them to forgive their birth parents for what they had done. I led them to bless their parents and ask God for an inheritance to be released from their bloodline. As we did this, the Spirit showed me a mantle of blessing falling on the right shoulder of Hannah, one of my leaders. I also led her to forgive her adopted parents for any offenses she held against them, to bless them, and to ask for her inheritance as well. I looked in the Spirit and saw a second mantle fall on Hannah's left shoulder. As I looked at the two mantles resting on her shoulders, I started to prophesy in the name of Jesus, "Satan has overplayed his hand one more time! If he had known what the final results of Calvary would be, he would have never crucified the Christ. He has done it again. He has overplayed his hand and succeeded in making a fatherless generation like never seen on earth. But I will release the Father's love to the fatherless, abandoned, and rejected generation and heal them. They will be the first generation with a legal right to a double portion and will become an army of harvesters."

> *Never pay back one wrong with another, or an angry word with another one: instead, payback with a blessing. That is what you are called to do, so that you inherit a blessing yourself. 1 Peter 3:9 (The Jerusalem Bible)*

This revelation of Sonship will release the former orphans to father their fathers. I believe this is the 11th hour worker in Matthew 20 with the legal right to a double portion. What Satan has tried to use as evil, God is going to use as a blessing.

After a time of prayer, Brother Casterline looked at me and asked, "Why do you keep coming to New York?" I said, "Because 16 years ago God showed me the wells of revival that have been capped in this city, dating back to the 1830's revival of Charles Finney. God said that He would give me a key that would unlock those wells, and that this city would see revival one more time." In the 1930s and 40s, flowing through the Bible school that Ivan Q. Spencer founded, there was a tremendous move of God. My mother actually got saved at one of their camp meetings, so I personally have a little skin in the game here. After the church and school moved, the city became very corrupt financially and morally dark. When spiritual leadership leaves a city or a region, there is usually a vacuum for either Godly leadership to emerge and replace them, or for the enemy to take over that place of authority.

Brother Casterline said, "I know that when the spiritual leadership of this school left the city, there were broken covenants and relationships among God's people. Now, I see that it has been an open door for the enemy to bring destruction, poverty, and moral decay to the city." I asked him to explain further in detail, and here's what he told me, "There was a young married girl who had an adulterous relationship with one of the students of the Bible school, and she became pregnant. Her family was in the leadership of this ministry. When the situation became public, they were asked to remove themselves. Therefore covenants were broken and a spiritual vacuum was left in this city." I asked him, "Dr. Casterline, how do you know this information?" He answered, "I am the bastard product of that relationship." God had just handed us some keys to unlock the old wells of revival. We started repenting for relationships, which had been broken over 60 years before, in the city where we both have responsibility and spiritual authority.

Brother Casterline told a story, during a message he was preaching, about how he had to overcome the shame that his mother carried her whole life. He said that she had a hard time looking at him without being reminded of the sin in which she had been involved when he was conceived. He saw her divorce papers with the words adultery stamped in red across the paper work. In the late 1950's that was a stigma that the enemy would use to beat up people who got divorced The cross and the blood applied to that curse will cancel it completely. Often, members of the body of Christ carry curses and burdens that are not necessary, but they affect inheritances. Brother Casterline would have never intentionally passed those curses to his children, but if they had not been addressed, they would have continued down the bloodline.

As I continued to travel to New York, God expanded my territory southward toward Pennsylvania. God showed me an hourglass, which started in Buffalo going east to Syracuse, south down to Hornell with the point down. He added a triangle with the point up, with points touching each other in Hornell and the base south all the way to highway 80 in Pennsylvania. The Lord told me to make a commitment to network with as many ministries and churches as I could, in order to bring enough unity to see a move of the Spirit. God used some old relationships to expand influence into Pennsylvania, and made some very strong relationships with business people who have a huge vision for the Kingdom. They are implementing it within their businesses and communities today.

I was just starting this new relationship of Sonship with Jack Taylor; my whole paradigm of the Gospel was shifting. A new realm of the Kingdom was starting to unfold before my very eyes. I spent much of 2010 and 2011 in New York. Most of the time, the honorariums didn't meet my expenses,. This had never been a problem in the past, but it was now, since I had closed my business, and fulltime ministry was our livelihood. It's amazing how that will influence what you say from the pulpit. When you need an offering to survive, you have a tendency to be a little nicer.

I was spending most of my time in New York, and because of my absence, my church in Florida was coming apart. I started to feel like a guest speaker there. During this time, the apostolic calling of birthing churches and covering them in relationship, was becoming a reality in my spirit. I would come back from a ministry trip with a fresh revelation and the zeal of a traveling evangelist, yet I couldn't make my own church function properly. At this point, I realized that the way it was going, I could not do both.

Greg and I had reached an impasse in our relationship, and we both knew we were in trouble. We had a confrontation one day when Greg came to me and told me that, for the first time ever, our visions were no longer the same. He pretty much accused me of changing my vision for One Kingdom Fellowship and our partnership. The vision hadn't changed, but my understanding of how the vision was to be facilitated had begun to evolve. With the accusation came a heated discussion...a boxing match. I called him on the carpet and told him he was unwilling to confront and solve situations in his own life and his family. He was unwilling to pay the price and deal with the issues that were holding him back from his true destiny. I yelled at him, letting him know that he wasn't man enough to admit it. I pointed out that he was actually the one who had completely lost his sense of purpose, and he needed to accuse me to take the heat away from himself. This was probably only the third time that Greg and I had been this loud and angry at each other in over 18 years. There's never been a man I've loved more than Greg. I remember pointing at him and screaming, "You lost your vision, and you want to blame me!" At the end of our argument, he said to me he knew the calling on my life. He told God if he was going to be a hindrance that he would back away. We hugged, kissed, and made up, before he left the office.

About three hours later I got a phone call from Greg's wife. Greg had been rushed to the hospital, his retina detached in his left eye. I immediately asked God to forgive me if I had any part to play in this situation. At that point we should have come to the conclusion that we were in trouble, but we both avoided dealing with what was wrong in our relationship. Our church was suffering. Some people who were close to us both knew that we were in trouble, but neither one of us would man up and deal with our issues. Greg and I both had been orphans for so long; we did not know how to address the root issues in both of our lives.

Jack Taylor was beginning to unlock my whole understanding of Sonship. I was experiencing a transformation that I never knew existed. One truth that I witnessed about Jack, that was different from anything I had known before, was his openness. On three different occasions Jack asked me to pray for him and father him in a few areas where he felt I had insight. I had never had that done to me before by any leader. Jack believes that we all can father each other with our strengths. I have personally watched Jack ask a man to father him. When this happened, I asked the Lord, "What did I just witness?" The Lord said, "It is the key to the Kingdom success in fathering."

Kingdom Key:
If you will focus on your own Sonship, your fathering will be empowered from Heaven.

I explained to the church body that I had a spiritual father named Jack Taylor. The desperate longing in my heart for approval and acceptance, along with some of the broken places in my emotions, were being healed. A group of members challenged me, believing that the Bible says that we are not permitted to call anyone father but God. They were in reality challenging my relationship with Papa Jack. They were so dogmatic about it, they left our church. I showed them in Scripture when apostle John often addressed people in this way in his letters, "To my little children." Looks like he thought he was their father. The apostle Paul talks about his sons Timothy and Titus, too. It's a theme that runs all through Scripture. By the way, God, the Father, spoke audibly from heaven at Jesus' baptism and said, "This is my Son in who I am well pleased." Look, Heaven is a mirror of what is to be done on earth. God is a Father, and I was finally starting to see Him in that image.

The first thing I wanted to do was get Jack Taylor to my church, because One Kingdom was hurting. I was hoping Jack would come and bring some unity. He was a true spiritual father to me, and I was hoping that the healing I had begun to feel would come to our church body as well.

I actually booked the date for Jack to come. After I booked a date with Jack, and as I was praying one morning, the Holy Spirit asked me why I hadn't asked Him if it was okay for Jack Taylor to come preach at my church. I had no clue that God would not approve of my new spiritual father preaching at my church. Then the Lord spoke clearly, "If you bring Jack Taylor into your fellowship, it will drive a wedge between you and Greg, one from which you two will never recover." He told me to call a friend of mine, Louis DeSiena in Jacksonville, and use that particular date for Jack to come up to his place instead. Jack was there for those dates; and Louis and his wife, Kathy, became the spiritual sons of Jack, too.

The weekend Jack Taylor and his son, Tim, went to speak at Louis's church, The Gate Fellowship in Jacksonville, I decided to get a hotel so we could all be together for the weekend. After that weekend with Tim and Jack, I realized that Jack had truly given me a place to sit at the table beside his natural son, and I actually had a place where my opinion mattered.

We planned a meeting in Firecreek, in the mountains outside of Asheville, North Carolina. Jack started to have Sons Gatherings there, and I was at the first one. It's a great place to share some family time! Firecreek is located in the Blue Ridge Mountains. There are three rustic homes hidden in a bowl shaped area with a pond in the middle. The main house has a big wraparound deck with a fireplace on it. The view alone is spectacular. In addition, Firecreek is a beautiful spot to have meetings because there are heavenly portals all over the land. Someone has redeemed the land as we are told to do in Joel 2:18. The Lord is zealous for His land, and pity His people who do not hold it sacred. If the robe I wear, combined with my righteousness, can turn filthy lucre into Kingdom cash, we can surely restore the land that God loves so much!

I have been to three Firecreek gatherings so far. The first time, I was still trying to figure out this sons thing and whether I had a place at the table or not. We sat around, built relationships, and told our stories. So I put it to the test, and became the open book that I am. I shared about my addiction to porn, how I date-raped my wife, how I had a gun and wanted kill the man who was with my wife. I was definitely trying to test this and make sure I truly had a place at Dad's table. The second time was a true blessing. Some relationships that were shaky and uncertain from the first time with some of my brothers, started to warm up a little, a true family dynamic began to emerge. If I have a father, then I have brothers. God is very serious about this family of His.

The third trip to Firecreek was the charm; relationships were sealed at this time. It changed me so much, I will make my sons or anyone that I have influence with, commit to at least two or three gatherings in order to get the full picture. Some have balked at this kind of commitment. These are the same people who complain about the people who come to their church a few times a year and don't get involved in real church family. Now that I have a little healing, orphans tick me off. You should have seen me when I stopped smoking! LOL.

I started planning a way to make sure that I got Greg around Papa Jack. Seven years ago, when I opened my lighting store in Vero Beach, I started a Bible study. I still go every couple of weeks on Wednesday morning at 8:00, which means I have to leave my house by 5:30 to get there. Greg and I would go to the Bible study with the businessmen in Vero Beach, and then spend the afternoon with Papa Jack. I did my very best to not interfere with Jack and Greg's relationship, so that it could be between them, and that he could get the healing that he needed.

You can only bring a horse to water, but you cannot make him drink.

About this time Randy, the man who left me his Harley, came back from China. We sat on my back porch chatting and he asked what had happened to me. He told me whatever I had gotten from God he wanted some. That day I prayed a father's blessing over Randy. The anointing was tangible to him, as much as it has been to me. Randy and I have been friends a long time, but we had no clue how this was going to work. I will have to explain it in a different book how this father son relationship works with two very strong prophets. That is a boxing match all by itself. Randy just happened to move to New York after he came back from China.

There was a shift going on. My understanding about this Sonship stuff, and the message I have been carrying for years about how to redeem the land, were starting to blend. In the process, it seemed that all my relationships were falling apart.

I was in New York and was asked to come to a meeting with some leaders of a ministry. A snowstorm hit that day. I was convinced that God had told me to go, so I went without Brother Casterline. It should have been a sign that when a local New Yorker won't travel on the roads, a Florida-born redneck shouldn't either.

The meeting could not have gone worse. I wept through most of it. I was being accused of trying to expand my ministry at the expense of their reputations and was asked to never mention their names within my circles of influence. This was extremely hurtful for me. I asked God, "What is going on with my ministry? If I keep doing it this way, I will not be successful." The Lord told me that He was proud of me, continually bringing fresh oil to others with the revelations He was showing me. He then said that not everybody wants to restore inheritances. It's a dirty job cleaning out the old capped wells; they are full of snakes and rocks. Most people don't have the spiritual guts to deal with all the trash that needs to be repented for. As I was driving back to Hornell in the worst snowstorm I have ever seen, the Lord told me that because of my obedience, I had gained favor with Him, even though I had not yet gained favor with man.

And Jesus increased in wisdom and stature, and in favor with God and men. Luke 2:52

He then told me that He would settle this for me in a prophetic dream that night. I was not to be worried about the religious people who rejected me.

When I went to bed, the Lord told me He was very pleased with how I was handling all that was going on. That night I had a vividly colored dream. I saw a 65 ft Hatteras fishing yacht with outriggers open. We were in the darkest blue waters I have ever seen, and Jesus was standing in the cockpit fishing. As I watched, Jesus was catching sailfish, white marlin, and blue marlin. They were all billfish. I saw Him catch about 40 different fish. Armed with a yellowish gold glove on His left hand, He dragged each fish up by the bill so he could whisper in the fish's ear, "Are you going to straighten up and fly right, or do I have to filet you?" With over half the fish, He would take the knife He had in His right hand, cut their throats and then put them in the fish box. The others He would release from the hook. As He released them, they would do a tail walk across the blue ocean water with what looked like joy because of their freedom. It was beautiful to watch. Jesus looked up and over His right shoulder, gazed directly into my eyes and deep into my soul, and started thanking me for taking Him fishing. He just kept telling me how much He loved to fish and thanked me.

I woke up and told Jesus, "I don't have a sport fishing boat anymore." I used to, but I couldn't see why He was thanking me for taking Him fishing now. Then the Lord said, "Oh, you didn't see the bait I was using." With that I went into a vision. Jesus was back in the boat showing me that I was the bait. He was thanking me for taking Him fishing because He loves to catch fish. He looked into my eyes and said, "I know it hurts when they bite, but they are the ones I am trying to hook, so I can heal them. Thanks for taking me fishing."

Kingdom Keys:

1. If you will focus on your own sonship, your fathering will be empowered from Heaven.

2. Jesus is a fisher of men. Are you mature enough for Him to use you as bait?

Round 14

Multiplication by Death

Verily, verily, I say unto you, Except a corn of wheat fall into the ground and die, it abideth alone: but if it die, it bringeth forth much fruit. John 12:24 (KJV)

In November 2011 I held a leadership meeting with all five of my church leaders. At this meeting, I offered three options:

Option #1: I would give Greg the 501c3 nonprofit tax exempt corporation, and all of the assets of the church. I would walk away and do nothing but itinerant ministry.

Option #2: Greg would give me complete control and walk away.

Option #3: I would take the senior leadership position privately and publicly. Greg would agree to that, and we would work out our differences and make this thing work with me as senior leader.

I gave all five of the leaders a 40 day window to make this decision. I told them I would honor and respect whatever decision they made. I stated that we should have done this 18 months ago, and that Greg and I were not even friends now, even though we were still friendly. One of the leaders looked to Greg and asked, "Is this true?" "Yes." He totally agreed and confessed that this was no longer working. I was going to a conference in Seattle and when I returned, they could tell me what they had decided.

No one made a decision within the 40 day window. Fifty-two days later, God invaded my bedroom one morning. He was not the sweet baby Jesus lying in a manger. God was angry with me! The Lord told me that I had jeopardized my own calling because of my love for Greg, and my lack of obedience to Him. Sternly, I was warned that if Greg and I did not separate now, there would never be an opportunity to reconnect properly in the future. With that I called Greg, weeping, and told him what the Lord said. Three days later he called me back, and agreed it was time.

Our first reaction was to just close the church. It was struggling financially and, truthfully, had become a royal pain. I was still having success with my Thursday night Bible studies, and had many spiritual sons traveling from as far as Orlando to meet with me. In my scramble to figure out what to do, we had a meeting with the leadership, again. At that time, all of them checked out, and were leaving One Kingdom except Don Kerr.

Here I was, yet again, having to make the hard decisions alone. It appeared as if the future of One Kingdom Fellowship was coming to an end, but I knew that I still needed to teach on Thursday evenings. I called Pastor Mark Gregory.

The Thursday morning between Christmas and New Year's was heartbreaking for me. I had lost every one, and I was hurting deep inside. As I prayed that morning, I could not voice what I needed from the Lord and felt lower than whale's poop. On the way to work, I started telling God that I wanted my mom. She always made things better. When I was seven, and God told her to rock me to sleep every night, she would prophesy over me and tell me Bible stories. My mother believed in me when no one else did.

As I arrived at the church that morning and slipped into my office, I felt an anointing enter the room. Out of the corner of my eye, I saw a spiritual being dressed in white linen walk into my office. For some reason I couldn't look at the face. I asked, "Is that You, Jesus?" He answered, "No." He asked, "Who were you asking for?" "My mother." I said. I looked at my mother's hand, and it was not crippled any more.

This was a different encounter than I have had before. I asked the Lord about this, and He said, "Heaven is starting to invade the earth's realm." I called Susie and explained what had just happened. I told her that the moment Mom came in, I knew that everything was going to be all right. She was one of the saints, dressed in white linen, and part of the great cloud of witnesses interceding for my inheritance to be fulfilled on the earth. Susie and I prayed together before I hung up the phone.

At 6:00 p.m., Hannah came to the church early for Bible study and wanted to see me. She asked me not to make fun of her, but she believed the Lord told her to demonstrate a prophetic act. She pulled up a chair and made me sit in her lap. She felt she represented my mother and that everything was going to be all right. Susie walked through the door while I was on Hannah's lap crying. She assumed, "You told her about what happened today." I had not. Hannah had no clue about her prophesy. I have no doubt that God is releasing all heaven for our benefit to redeem our inheritance.

Let me explain that I was not communicating with the dead like Deuteronomy 18:10-13 talks about. If you believe the rapture is your escape route, you will probably believe this is wrong. If you think Jesus is sending the great cloud of witness to start changing the realm of the Kingdom, so that the bridegroom can come for His bride without spot or wrinkle, you will start accessing the realms of Heaven that are available to us.

The next day, I went to the breakfast meeting that had been arranged with Pastor Mark, and asked him if he could help meet some of my needs. I was hoping to use his facility on Tuesday nights to rebuild the leadership, and on Thursday nights for a Bible study. As I laid out my plans, Pastor Mark totally agreed with no hesitation, and made it extremely affordable. When I was finished, Mark looked at me and asked, "Is that all you wanted?" "Yes," I replied.

Mark asked me if the Lord had shown me anything about him and his wife doing ministry with me. To my amazement, he shared that he and Phyllis had known for years that they were supposed to submit to me in ministry. He proposed blending the two churches under my leadership, submitting to me as the apostle and senior leader. It could prove to be a double blessing since Phyllis is probably the best children's minister in the county. The bottom line was that they were willing to submit to me and be my associates, if I would have them. The Lord reminded me of the dream that Greg's wife had. In this case, this couple was willing to come and to fill any role that the church needed.

Only God could bring these kinds of things together. There was definite room for bitterness between us from our dealings in the past. At one time they had been my pastors, but I wound up with a financial blessing in a building that they chose to leave. However, they still had the ability to hear God and try to follow Him. With lots of decisions to be made on all sides, it was a crazy Christmas season for all of us. There were lots of options, and no concrete decisions had been made yet. There I was on January 2, 2012 standing out in front of the church looking at a building I could not afford and asking God what to do.

The Holy Spirit bellowed at me, and here's what He said, "I finally have you right where I want you, by yourself, completely surrendered to me. You have no one to turn to and that is by My design. You made covenants with people to cover your weaknesses. You made covenants that usurped the covenant with your wife. You've been bellyaching, whining for her to stand up, and to take her rightful place, but you never made room for her because of covenants that you had made with others. You need to break all of them and make room for her to stand beside you and lead this ministry as a team." He gave me instructions on how to deal with the landlord who owned the building. He showed me two triangles and told me that Mark and Phyllis's church was one triangle and the remnant of One Kingdom Fellowship was the other triangle. He said that He was going to give me the grace to blend the two. I'd like to tell you that we didn't lose any people, but we did. Everyone's wagon got turned upside down.

Don Kerr was the remaining leader who didn't walk out, but when Don heard that Mark and Phyllis were going to join us, he demonically manifested. He started cussing me out on the phone. "So, when you're preaching in New York, who is going to be in charge?" He wigged out and temporarily lost his mind. Don had spent a few years in prison because of this kind of behavior, and I'd had enough. Don demanded, "Who is going to be in charge, me or Mark?" He started giving me all this "I have been faithful" garbage. So I finished cleaning house with Don. It was official; I was totally leaderless. Only me. I was all alone. About 90 minutes later, Don called back like always and repented. I thought I was done, but the Lord told me this would bring a healing that would last. It had better, because I was mad.

The next day Don came to the church, and we talked. He started repenting to me, and confessed how bad he felt for the way he cussed me. He still tried to justify himself, because I was his spiritual father. It hurt and made him angry that Mark would be in charge, and he was being overlooked. I asked, "What did your father do to you at four years old?" He said, "I love my Dad." I said, "What did he do to you at four years old?" He said it again, "I love my Dad." "DON!" He started yelling, "I hate my father! I hate my father! But I want to love him. I led him to the Lord before he died." I saw a large angel holding a yellow cordless screw gun. Attached to it was a 36" metal shaft with claw-like barbs on it. (You've seen the TV ad to remove weeds in the garden. It was like one of those things.) He pushed it into Don's chest. We heard the most grueling screams when the angel pulled out this demon that had been in Don's heart since he was four years old.

As I started to pray, both Don and I saw a man dressed in white linen enter the room. I asked, "Jesus is that You?" He said, "No, it's Don's father. He has been trading on the trading floors of heaven for Don's deliverance and is now here to bless him with a father's blessing." This encounter has changed both Don's life and mine. God is doing some great things!

I can tell you that blending two systems together is not easy. I had a group of people who have walked with me, some of them almost four years. They understood the Kingdom lifestyle that I taught. Now we had another group who were entrenched in church doctrine and while very good at keeping the anointing in the church, were pretty much clueless about how the Kingdom functions. So, the Kingdom thinkers, who thought they were real spiritual, got upset that I would give a place to the old religious system, and they became meaner than the old church system people.

I felt like I was in the middle of an old, wild west shoot out. One triangle was shooting at the other one, and both were standing on what they claimed to be Biblical principles. The church people claimed that I had no structure, wouldn't exercise authority, and force people to submit and behave themselves. The super spiritual Kingdom group would whisper that I really didn't understand the Kingdom as much as I claimed to. I would overhear in the spirit realm that all my wounding had blinded my revelation.

By now, I asked God for permission to kill everyone and let me throw in the towel! Instead, He used it as a great teaching tool for me. The Lord told me to explain to those who would listen that in the Spirit these thoughts, attitudes, and influences were word curses. The curses came in the form of arrows and were penetrating the hearts of the brothers and sisters in the body. Now, this wasn't some demonic activity from the outside. These were Christians speaking curses with their words. The damage was coming from the inside. One triangle system was shooting at the other triangle system. Both claimed to have the Word of the Lord on their side and the authority to stand and exercise judgment. If we're not careful, all of us get caught up and do this.

It became obvious that Mark and Phyllis felt like they did not fit into our system, whatsoever. They were prepared to leave. This was a tough season for me, because I had sworn that I would not tolerate what happened in the last season. I would deal quickly with issues and not let them fester, like I had in the past. But the Holy Spirit told me to be quiet. He showed me that some of the leadership, who had come over with Mark and Phyllis, had picked up the Kingdom message.

One of their leaders, Rodney, received the Kingdom principles. When he informed me that Mark and Phyllis were planning to leave, God told me to tell Rodney to help solve the problem because of the long relationship that he had with Mark and Phyllis. I told him that I was prepared to be thrown under the bus and be the scapegoat, if it was necessary. But at all costs, I wanted to try and bring healing to them, and let them know that God chose them. I did not choose them. He was to reinforce the fact that I loved them, and believed that God was in the middle of this merger. Rodney was amazed at my willingness to be wrong, so others could get right. We all eventually were able to sit down, work out our hurts and wounds, and the frustrations.

Kingdom key:
In the church, people model what you do.
In the Kingdom you reproduce who you are.

After this crisis, the Lord spoke to me and said, "I told you to make covenant with them. Explain your value of covenant to them and tell them that the covenant has now been tested." Now let us find our rightful places in the Kingdom and build this church properly. I desperately needed both of their giftings, but in this area of my own sonship and understanding, I was no longer going to jeopardize my role as the senior leader. As I finish writing this chapter, we are about to celebrate our one-year anniversary together.

In the midst of this crisis, I truly had come to the end of my rope. I was sitting in my office at the church, where I have a picture of the triangle up system and a picture of the triangle down system on one wall, and on the front wall of my office I have a picture of the Star of David with Jesus in the middle. In Genesis 25:21-24, we read:

> *Now Isaac pleaded with the Lord for his wife, because she was barren: and the Lord granted his plea, and Rebekah his wife conceived. But the children struggled together within her: and she said, if all is well why am I like this? So she went to inquire of the Lord. And the Lord said to her: "two nations are in your womb, two people shall be separate from your body: one people shall be stronger than the other, and the older shall serve the younger." So when her days were fulfilled for her to give birth, indeed there were twins in her womb.*

As the Lord started revealing to me what the Scriptures were saying, He showed me that Rebekah had been barren for over 20 years. I am just now coming into my 20th year of serving the Lord Jesus Christ. But Isaac prayed for Rebekah, and she finally conceived. She thought that her days of rejection from the Lord were over, since once you conceived in that culture all was supposed to be well. Like Rebekah, I know I have been pregnant with a promise and a blueprint from heaven, but there's been a boxing match going on inside of my spiritual womb, just like hers. When she inquired of the Lord, she was told by Him, to endure the boxing match going on inside, and that the older would serve the younger. As I sat and pondered, "What are you showing me?" Jesus came to me and visited me with tears in His eyes. He said, "Charlie, please do not abort the babies that you're carrying." I pleaded with the Lord for some supernatural prenatal care, because it felt like I was trying to birth two rhinoceroses backwards. Then at that very moment, I felt the grace of His love totally engulf me.

The boxing match has been both painful and beneficial, but I believe that we are on the right road for both systems to function together. I think that the older system of the church *will become a foundation for the Kingdom to manifest God's Glory.* The Lord's Prayer says it best, *"Our Father who art in heaven, Hallowed be Thy name, Thy Kingdom come. Thy will be done on earth, as it is in heaven."*

How can we bring heaven to earth when we do not know how to operate in the heavenly realms? Authority in the heavenly realms is through Sonship, not just with an earthly father like Papa Jack, or by becoming spiritual fathers. We gain authority by going into the heavenly Kingdom. Our rightful inheritance is seeing Papa God face-to-face. Under the law you couldn't see God face to face, but under grace we can.

Kingdom Key:
Grace is to be a positive empowerment for righteousness, not a defensive excuse for sin.

Kingdom Keys:

1. In the church, people model what you do. In the Kingdom people reproduce who you are.

2. Under the law, man and God never met face-to-face, but in the Kingdom they do.

3. Because of the cross of Jesus Christ there is no greater sin than to commit the sin that was committed against you.

4. Grace is to be a positive empowerment for righteousness, not a defensive excuse for sin.

Round 15

Bringing Heaven to Earth

I thoroughly enjoy the revelation of sonship, and my relationship with my spiritual father, Jack Taylor. God has used this revelation to release fresh anointing and healing within my life. I'm sure that many have felt as if I have become a fanatic over this message of Sonship. Like Mary, who wiped Jesus' feet with her tears because she was so happy to have her sins forgiven, so I too have rejoiced in, promoted and reproduced what Papa Jack has given me. I now have personal sons and daughter-sons who are finding the healing that I have and are starting to walk out their relationship with God at a much deeper level. In my pursuit for revival, I found God as a Father! As I started to walk in my own Sonship, God revealed to others that I was a spiritual father. It's like a neon sign over my head was turned on that read, "Father, open for business."

One night Ron, an 84-year-old who had been coming to my Thursday night Bible study, came up to me after the meeting and handed me a note asking if I would be his spiritual father. He said that he had been looking for me for over 68 years. I have several sons from that generation, who have never been spiritually fathered. I have found in the church system that the fathers choose the sons, and then in most cases mold then to look and act just like them. I believe that in the Kingdom, the sons will pick the fathers as the Spirit highlights them.

Ladies, you are sons. If I can be the bride, you can be sons in the Kingdom. Coming to terms with the roles women play in ministry today has been a growth process for me. I had to undo quite a bit of religious teaching that had been ingrained in me. I was taught that women could not be preachers much less be apostles. It was a life changing experience when I had to buy a $125 army jacket, put five stars on it, give it to a female leader, and then publicly declare she was an apostle. After I allowed this revelation to change my ability to help fulfill their destinies, I have seen the apostolic gifting on many women. I have always believed that the role of the apostle is the fathering gift of the fivefold ministry.

I was in New York doing some regional meetings and prophesied over a woman. I was sure I could see the ministry gift of the apostle on her life and was speaking about what I saw. The Lord showed me that she had gone even deeper in the process of the Kingdom than I had. He showed me that she had a set of spiritual testicles. Her true calling was the ability to reproduce the Kingdom as a spiritual father, and this would develop as she pursued Sonship. This revelation has come through the process of seeing the Lord's army of women who will be instrumental in this revival and great harvest.

Some of Satan's twisted attacks on women in ministry have been over the ability to reproduce with seed. In Genesis 3:15, God said that the seed of the woman would bruise the head of Satan. The Kingdom seed, that a woman has, is the prophetic gifting of the word of God. In the Kingdom, women have spiritual seed just like the men do, so fathering is not a male-only gender club. I will give more details in the book "Women with Kingdom Seed." Too many woman have had to fight for their rightful place in the body, but if they stop after they are confirmed as apostles and don't complete the journey to Sonship, they will build a ministry on their gifting and not the Kingdom family. When we wear the robe of Sonship that Jesus gives us, we position ourselves to also become spiritual fathers, both male and female.

I asked the Lord, "How do I keep this father-son relationship pure and not create a network or create another "ism" worse than denominationalism?" He told me that if I have as many sons from outside my church as within, I would stay balanced. This is not building a mountain to me, and will keep me pure with true Kingdom DNA. With that formula, God spoke to me about my spiritual son, Brad, and showed me that I had brought a lot of healing to him. He said to go speak to Apostle Fowler in Orlando, and send Brad off to serve him in his church. This is Kingdom fathering. I had taken Brad as far as my personal gifting could take him, so although I am still fathering Brad, he is serving under Apostle Fowler.

Kingdom Key:
If people are your greatest asset, what better seed to sow for the best harvest?

A CEO or a director of an orphanage would never send a strong leader who is faithful and a good tither to assist someone else, except as punishment. (Why is it always the good givers?) A generous father will release a son to complete the training that is required to be successful in the Kingdom. You can only reproduce who you are, so that puts God back in the driver's seat, and it keeps this father/son paradigm pure.

A little over a year ago, I took a road trip and went to several of my cousins' houses on the east coast from Florida to New York. One by one, I started sharing the power of the father's blessing with them. Many of us who were raised in church, watched our fathers and mothers who were leaders, serve God with their whole hearts. There was something missing in our fathers' generation. None of us had ever received a father's blessing. As I finished this trip, I wound up in New York at my sister's house. I called my father and asked, "Dad, how is it that your generation completely missed the power of the father's blessing?" His answer completely shocked me. He said, "Charlie, some things you have to earn." I asked, "Dad, what Bible have you been reading?" I told him that was bogus, and a son should never have to earn his father's blessing. I hung up on him, and told God I was not going to fight with him any longer about this.

Three weeks later on a Monday morning, the Holy Spirit told me to call my father, and repent for being angry with him. I was in no frame of mind to discuss it any longer with him. I told God that if He couldn't get his attention, I was no longer going to try to deal with him. About two hours later, the Holy Spirit prompted me again; "Call your father to discuss this matter with him." I told God that if He couldn't talk to him, convince him that he was wrong, and have him call me, there'd be no call, because I refused to fight with him any longer.

At about five o'clock that afternoon, I got a phone call from the emergency room of the hospital. My 85-year-old father had been riding his bicycle and was hit by a truck going 55 miles per hour. He was airlifted to the trauma center 30 miles away. I immediately asked the Lord if I had caused the situation. He informed me that I told Him to get my dad's attention, because I refused to deal with him any longer. At that moment I went into a vision, and was shown the symbolism of the accident. The Lord told me that Dad was going to be okay. He would not have any broken bones, and I did not need to go until 3:00 p.m. the next day to see him. As I walked into his hospital room, the doctors were just leaving, amazed that he had no broken bones. I sat down next to my dad and told him that I had a word from the Lord. He interrupted me, "Before you get started, I need to talk to you about the phone call we had a few weeks ago, I've been meaning to call you and tell you that I was wrong." Those are words I'd not heard much from him.

I started talking to him about the prophetic symbols that God had shown me about his accident. A large extended cab white truck represented the corporate ministry vehicle. My father and uncles, who were leaders in the past, were riding in it. My father was riding his bicycle, which represents the ministry that he is now doing in the prison systems. When the mirror of the large truck struck him in the back of the head and threw him into the middle of a highway, the paramedics had to cut his clothes off to find the trauma, and then, airlift him to the hospital for healing. I explained to my dad that the mirror was looking at the history of what had been accomplished in the church system. It threw him into the highway, representing humanity, to expose the wounds of the past system, in which he was a leader. I told my dad that he needed to choose to help me in ministry and heal the wounds from the system, where he used to be a leader. My dad received the revelation and said to me, "Listen, I will do what ever you tell me to do. Just don't get me killed!"

Several months later I had spent the weekend with my dad, and when I got home, he called me. He said, "Charlie, you have offended me this weekend." I wondered, "How did I offend you this time, Dad?" He said, "You keep insinuating that I am a spiritual orphan." I said, "Dad, I want to be extremely blunt with you and tell you this. You are one of the worst spiritual orphans I have ever seen." His answer shocked me! I expected another round of boxing with him like I have had most of my life when we talk about the Kingdom. He said this to me, "Well, when are you going to man up, pray a father's blessing over me, and break this thing off of my life?" As I prayed a father's blessing over my own father, I felt the heavens themselves begin to open. I don't know if it did anything for him personally at that moment, but the fulfillment of what my mother had told me on her deathbed was starting to come into alignment with the Kingdom. Sometimes you don't know what God is doing till you see the results.

A week later in prayer, the Holy Spirit gave me a revelation about Central Assembly in Vero Beach that had been started from the church split over 40 years ago. I called my Dad with the revelation that God had given me, and started to explain it. He stopped me and said this, "Charlie, I don't have a clue what you're trying to show me. But I trust you, and I know that it's God. Call Pastor Buddy and make an appointment. Tell me where to be, what time to be there, and I'll do whatever you ask me to do." With that, I called Pastor Buddy and made an appointment. My father is the only living deacon who was part of the leadership from over 40 years ago; he carries the legal responsibility of the broken relationships that occurred under their watch. Many times while cleansing the land in the regions of New York and Florida, I have had to repent for sins that were many generations old. When my father, still alive, repents and then blesses, it releases a double portion. As I watched these two giants in the Kingdom ask not only each other's forgiveness but also the organizations they represented, I felt the anointing of the Holy Spirit. I had brought a basin of water and a towel. Together as a father/son team, my father and I washed Pastor Buddy's feet. We even anointed his feet with perfume. Finally, my father prayed a blessing over him. Something happened that day in the Kingdom that I cannot explain. When my father got in the car with me, he said to me, "Your mother's prophecy has now been fulfilled. I believe you're a man of God, and I will serve you."

The Lord has shown me that when the generation of a father can submit to the generation of the son, there is a double portion anointing that comes on them both. The Lord showed me that the body of Christ has been a generation behind the world, as exampled by Ishmael and Isaac. Ishmael had 12 sons and became a nation. Isaac had 2 sons. Jacob, the next generation, had 12 sons and became the nation of Israel. The key to overcoming this gap begins with the older generation of the church, while still alive and in her prime, submitting to the younger generation, and blessing it. The body of Christ can then walk in a double portion anointing and become the head, not the tail in all areas of life, not just within the walls of the church building.

The seven mountains of influence on the earth today are there for our taking. If we will operate with Kingdom principles, we can have the influence to rule on earth and not only in the heavens. Those mountains of influence are: media, government, education, economy, celebration, religion, and family. It is the kingdom of earth vs. the Kingdom of heaven. We were created to rule and reign with Him in heaven and bring it to earth. We are commanded to pray, "Thy Kingdom come, Thy will be done, on earth as it is in heaven." Look what the prophets say about our role as sons:

> *Thus says the Lord of hosts: 'If you will walk in My ways, And if you will keep My command, Then you shall also judge My house, And likewise have charge of My courts; I will give you places to walk Among these who stand here. Zechariah 3:7*

In the midst of this wrangling with my father, I asked God two questions: 1) *If I am supposed to govern (or judge) the church with Kingdom principles on earth, what is the structure in which I am to function?* 2) *If I'm supposed to have charge over the courts in heaven, what is the formula, and how do I execute it with the right protocols?* With all the strife and rumbling that went on between the two systems within my own church,

God finally gave me the answers to both questions. In a vision I walked into my office at church. On the credenza behind my desk, I have five baseball hats labeled: Apostle, Prophet, Evangelist, Pastor, and Teacher. As I walked in, I saw these five hats. I walked behind my desk and took off my crown of Sonship and placed it on my desk. Then I leaned my King scepter in the corner, and removed my priestly robe that I was wearing. I turned, grabbed the five hats and went out into the main sanctuary. I started teaching the people how to come into the unity of the faith and become mature in their own Sonship, and how to function in the Kingdom realm as Sons, Kings, and Priests.

When we bring the two triangles together properly, we will bring heaven to earth. All of the struggling and fighting that has taken place has been for one simple reason; I have been fighting for my true inheritance, as we all do. I finally have the answer about why I never fit in any of the systems or networks where God told me to submit. They were good and God is using them, but they never had the transference of inheritance of the Kingdom DNA that I was looking for. Ephesians 4:11-13 holds the key for me:

And He Himself gave some to be apostles, some prophets, some evangelists, and some pastors and teachers, for the equipping of the saints for the work of ministry, for the edifying of the body of Christ, till we all come to the unity of the faith and of the knowledge of the Son of God, to a perfect man, to the measure of the stature of the fullness of Christ...

The first thing I noticed was that the fivefold ministry is temporary. It will eventually become obsolete, when the body of Christ comes into the fullness of its maturity. I am not planning to walk through the pearly gates one day, look at God and say, "Hey, Apostle Charlie is here, or Prophet Doodad is here." No! I will be welcomed as a son by my heavenly Father. I have come to the conclusion that the same robe that Jesus put on me, the one that has empowered me to live a holy life and given me boldness to exercise authority over my family, is also the robe of Sonship. Jesus was a Priest and Son, and He carried all fivefold gifts. But He was also a King. I will be wearing my robe of righteousness, which has the dual robe of Sonship when I get to heaven.

Look at the word *equipping*, "katartismos" in the Greek. Strong's number for this word is 2677. It is defined as, "to make to fit, to prepare, train, perfect, make fully qualified for service." The Great Physician is now making all the necessary adjustments so the Church will not be "out of joint."

Look at the word *perfect*, "teleios" in the Greek. It has Strong's number 5466. It refers to "that which has reached an end, that is, finished, complete, and perfect." When applied to people, the word perfect is used in Ephesians. Four signifies consummate soundness, and includes the idea of being whole. More particularly, when applied to believers, it denotes *maturity*.

I was created in God's image, which means I was created a "spirit being."

God is Spirit, and those who worship Him must worship in spirit and truth. John 4:24

In order to enter the Kingdom and function as the spiritual son that I am, I have to come to the end of myself, allowing Christ to complete the finished work that He did on the cross, making me whole.

In John 3, Jesus told Nicodemus that he must be born again to see the Kingdom. Watch what Jesus said, and also what Jesus did not say. He said Nicodemus could see the Kingdom. He did not say that he was in the Kingdom. It was only available to him if he was willing to pay the price of surrender, and to come to the end of himself, which is spiritual MATURITY. I know a lot of people who are born-again, but have no clue about the Kingdom. It's through the dying of our flesh and the maturing of our understanding, that we enter the Kingdom and then find our rightful place among those who walk there.

My true inheritance is to function as a Son, King, and Priest. A spirit being, within the Kingdom realm under these functions, brings heaven to earth. He then uses the fivefold ministry gifts to bring the body of Christ into the unity of faith and maturity in their Sonship. We are to model the father/son paradigm as a family, which is a mirror image of the way it is in heaven. We function accordingly:

as a **Son**: To be about the Father's business.

as a **King**: To take charge of His courts and to judge His house.

as a **Priest**: To make sure we bring the proper sacrifices through intercession that is pleasing to the Father in both realms, heavenly and earthly.

As I started to be thankful to God for bringing me to maturity, He asked if I trusted Him. (That's not a good sign). I had proven I was willing to pay whatever price it took to receive my inheritance and to know the promises of revival. I had to work through the natural inheritance with my son Bryan when I was painting his new house, that he bought with the money he saved while in Iraq. I was painting alone in the house and feeling a little sad. I was limited to doing manual labor and couldn't write checks the way I used to. God spoke and said; "Bryan's blessing is from your inheritance to him. Good job." I told God, "Thanks, but that doesn't impress me. What about natural inheritance?" God spoke, "What would you like to give him as a sign that you're proud of him." I said, "Lord, he has a new car. He and Lori are married and have a beautiful little girl, Madison. They are blessed. If I had money like I had previously, I would give him a boat to enjoy with his family like we used to." "OK, I will handle it," He offered. Then He asked, "If you're so concerned about making sure of the natural inheritance versus the spiritual, you know Jason is also living from your blessing. What about him? What do you want him to have?" I could feel this one coming from the inside and confessed, "The Rolex? No, not my Rolex! But God, it was a sign that revival was coming." I then let God know that if He wanted me to give my Rolex to Jason, I would, but to have Susie confirm it.

That night we were talking about ministry in New York, and Susie said, "The Rolex has been a sign to you, but it doesn't mean what it used to. You should give it to Jason. He likes good watches." There's your sign, redneck—Jason took the Rolex and thanked me for it.

The next day Reggie Parker came into the office with a large blue boat bumper that keeps boats from slamming into the dock. He told me that God was about to give me a buffer to help me not to slam into the dock any more. Then he gave me the title to a boat that I had given him several years ago. The Lord told him to sow it back into my life. I was able to give it to Bryan as a gift from me to welcome him home from the army.

Man, I wished I had never had this inheritance burden come on me. I bankrupted my company, and had several buildings that I had to let go back to the bank. I planned to retire with millions. Now, God was telling me to put the New York ministry on the altar. The church was nothing but a pain, I had my own boat repossessed, and Jason got my watch. In the midst of my self-pity God asks, "Do You trust Me?" "God, I am getting mad! I am calling a family meeting!" I told the Lord, "This sucks! All I get is a stupid promise with a blue boat bumper, and a word that You're going to help keep me from slamming into docks. I am getting frustrated with promises. I want my stuff back. God, I feel like a "dirt ball." Then the Holy Spirit reminded me that 18 years before Jason had told me I was turning this family into dirt balls. He started telling me that my family trusted me when they felt like dirt balls, but they followed me as I followed God. Now they have the ability to hear God's voice and have a relationship with Him. The Father was proud of me and I was maturing in my walk. The journey has been hard, but yes, I trust you, PAPA.   I heard the Father say, "Welcome to 'begotten Sonship;' this is your true inheritance."   I was puzzled and inquired, "Jesus, what is begotten Sonship?" "A 'begotten son' is one who is ruled by the single thought, 'what does the Father want?' He is one who is willing to die at the hands of others and walk in love, so that the Father gets the credit," He told me. A begotten son allows the Father the opportunity of loving him, instead of giving him what he deserves.   We all know John 3:16:

For God so loved the world that He gave His only begotten Son, that whoever believes in Him should not perish but have everlasting life.

The Greek word for *begotten* is "monogenes." It has Strong's number G3439 and means "a single gene." *Mono*=single and *Gen*=to cause to "gen"-erate. The DNA of God is *Christ in you, the hope of Glory.* When this Kingdom seed is the prominent focus, the Kingdom of heaven and the kingdom of earth kiss in the form of the Father's love.

I asked the Lord what test I passed to advance to this level. He said, "Like Abraham, you were willing to sacrifice your promise." (In Abraham's case it was his son; in mine it was the promise of revival.) "I knew I could trust you. Even when others don't agree, you have tried to obey Me. I also love your willingness to take Me fishing and let Me use you as the bait," He said. Then I heard the Father pronounce over me, "This is my Son in Whom I am well pleased." Let's expand the kingdom!!

Kingdom Keys:

1. In my pursuit of revival I found God as a Father!

2. If people are your greatest asset, what better seed to sow for the best harvest?

Round 16

The Power of Redeemed Orphans!

"Women who behave, rarely make history"

Last year in obedience to the Lord, I stopped traveling to New York. I have gone through a death process concerning all the promises of revival. In that process I have found God to be a Father in new and personal ways. My church has also been merging as a family, and new things are happening between Susie and me.

We were blessed with a condo on the beach for a few weeks. During that time I realized I had been promoted in the Kingdom. I told Susie things were changing. The night before I asked God if I had found favor with Him, and if so, man, I wanted a new Rolex. I didn't want the one I had given to Jason. I wanted God to give me a new one, at least a blue-faced submariner or one of the several others that I like. (I like nice watches.) A few days later Jason came up to work on his rental house. He called Susie and told her he had left my Rolex on the dresser. He felt like that was what he was supposed to do. I had wanted a new one, but God showed me how the son was giving his inheritance back to his father. Sounds a lot like family doesn't it.

A few weeks later I was preparing to go to Louis DeSiena's church in Jacksonville. I asked the Lord, "What am I to preach on, and what am I to bring to their church?" He started to review with me all the different anointings I have carried into a city or church. Sometimes I have brought the prophet, apostle or even the evangelist. This time the Lord said, "I have a new mantle of anointing for you to bring to Jacksonville. You are bringing the anointed mantle of a brother. You are the brother of Louis and Kathy, bringing a brother's love to them and the anointing of a rich uncle to their church body. This was a totally new anointing for me, and we had a great meeting. This family thing in the Kingdom is real.

A few weeks ago I was preaching on God being a Father. I was sharing the fight I had against my beliefs of how God functions as a father, because my experience in the natural was one of living with a strict father, who taught we had to earn love. Right in the middle of my message, Susie came and took the microphone. She began to explain how her opinion of God the Father was different from mine. She told the church that when she got pregnant at 16 years old, her father came to her bedside, told her that he was sorry for what had happened to her, and he would stand beside her. He told her that there was nothing she could do that would make him ashamed of her. She started to tell the congregation, "That's how God the Father is. There is nothing that you have done or could do that would make Him ashamed of you. Nothing!" The power of God hit the room. For over an hour, Susie prayed for people who came down front and laid hands on them.

Later that day, as we talked about what happened, Susie said that it's only been the last few years that she believed we served the same God. Susie and I serve the same God, but too much of the time, I only showed one side. God is Love, and that has to be the foundation. When the foundation of Love supports the archway of Honor, a door of God's Favor will open to you. After 20 years of trying on my own, I believe that I am just now starting to walk in my true ministry calling. Thanks, Mom, for giving a word from God that kept Dad and me in the ring fighting long enough to find the Kingdom and the Father.

I was given a word from the Lord: *The assignment of Obadiah has come to an end.* He spoke that same word to me for over a week every morning. *The assignment of Obadiah has come to an end.* I read the whole book of Obadiah a few times, but it meant nothing to me. So I inquired a little more about what God was showing me, and He said, "Obadiah was the servant of Ahab and Jezebel."

And Ahab had called Obadiah, who was in charge of his house. (Now

Obadiah feared the Lord greatly. For so it was, while Jezebel massacred the prophets of the Lord, that Obadiah had taken one hundred prophets and hidden them, fifty to a cave, and had fed them with bread and water.) 1Kings 18:3-4

The assignment of Obadiah has come to an end. Tell the prophets who are hiding in the caves that it's time to clean up from sloppy cave living and prepare to find their rightful place in the Kingdom.

I saw a vision of a mountain where the prophets were hiding in the very back of the cave as far away from the opening as they could get. I then saw wives, pastors, and Christian leaders trying to drag them back into the church system with words of rebuke, shame and manipulation. To get away from the old system, they ran as far as they could go, to the thin, back wall of the cave. I was watching this from a viewpoint where I could see the whole mountain. The cave opening was the old church system. The Lord spoke to me, "Tell them they will not go back into what was old, but they are to prepare to emerge into the Kingdom." Then I saw three angels with C-4 plastic explosive set charges outside the cave's thin, back wall. As the explosives detonated, an opening was made for the prophets to emerge into the Kingdom.

For Jesus Himself testified that a prophet has no honor in his own country. John 4:44

The assignments of Obadiah and Abraham Lincoln have now come to an end. We need to find our rightful places within the Kingdom. Susie has a quote on the fridge that I like: *"Women who behave, rarely make history."* I have always looked to the Bible for my life lessons and have found that God has done some of His best work, many times, with redeemed orphans and slaves. So as we look at Scripture, there is no excuse for you or me to remain broken, not receive the blessing of healing, and not become whole. We can have a double portion, if we're willing to fight for what is rightfully ours. Look at Jephthah's journey in Judges 11:1-8:

Now Jephthah the Gileadite was a mighty man of valor, but he was the son of a harlot; and Gilead begot Jephthah. Gilead's wife bore sons; and when his wife's sons grew up, they drove Jephthah out, and said to him, "You shall have no inheritance in our father's house, for you are the son of another woman." Then Jephthah fled from his brothers and dwelt in the land of Tob; and worthless men banded together with Jephthah and went out raiding with him. It came to pass after a time that the people of Ammon made war against Israel. And so it was, when the people of Ammon made war against Israel, that the elders of Gilead went to get Jephthah from the land of Tob. Then they said to Jephthah, "Come and be our commander, that we may fight against the people of Ammon." So Jephthah said to the elders of Gilead, "Did you not hate me, and expel me from my father's house? Why have you come to me now when you are in distress?" And the elders of Gilead said to Jephthah, "That is why we have turned again to you now, that you may go with us and fight against the people of Ammon, and be our head over all the inhabitants of Gilead."

Jephthah, a son of a harlot, rejected and willing to fight for his rightful inheritance, became a captain of the ones who stole his birthright. Abraham had to leave his father's house and go to a land that God would show him. He had to deal with family issues, then he had to put his promise on the altar, so God would know that he trusted Him. Moses's mother had to float his assets, so he could be adopted by Pharaoh's daughter; however, when his true inheritance came into view, he reacted with zeal, and was banished to the desert for 40 years to be de-orphan-ized of his orphan spirit. His wife called him a bloody husband. Ultimately, he got his reward.

By faith Moses, when he became of age, refused to be called the son of Pharaoh's daughter, choosing rather to suffer affliction with the people of God than to enjoy the passing pleasures of sin, esteeming the reproach of Christ greater riches than the treasures in Egypt; for he looked to the reward. (Inheritance) Hebrews 11:24-26

Church Fathers vs. Kingdom Sons

David was considered to be illegitimate or at the least rejected by the family by many scholars, but David had the insight of the Kingdom. When he fought Goliath, there was a key to David's victory. Goliath asked for a man to fight. David showed up as a Spirit-son and kicked his butt. David wrote in Psalms, *"Do not take Your Holy Spirit from me,"* a thousand years before the veil was torn and the Holy Spirit released.

Joseph was sold as a slave, helped recover the family inheritance, and was willing to lay his life down for his family. He received a robe and ring, but never sandals. (Slaves didn't get sandals.) He died a slave, reproduced who he was, and enslaved Israel, and then the whole nation of Egypt where Pharaoh owned everything. His two sons, Ephraim and Manasseh were listed with the 12 tribes of Israel and a double portion was released.

Moses took off his sandals at the burning bush. He was doing what Boaz did to redeem Elimelech and Naomi's lost inheritance. They had been looking for the true inheritance, His presence.

> *Then Boaz said, "On the day you buy the field from the hand of Naomi, you must also buy it from Ruth the Moabitess, the wife of the dead, to perpetuate the name of the dead through his inheritance." And the close relative said, "I cannot redeem it for myself, lest I ruin my own inheritance. You redeem my right of redemption for yourself, for I cannot redeem it." Now this was the custom in former times in Israel concerning redeeming and exchanging, to confirm anything: one man took off his sandal and gave it to the other, and this was a confirmation in Israel. Ruth 4:5-7*

In Genesis 38, Tamar was looking for her inheritance. Onan only stimulated Tamar and didn't impregnate her, because he spilled the Kingdom seed on the ground. God killed Onan for his disrespect of the Kingdom seed. The church has been good at stimulation. Tamar later found out that Judah was still cheating her out of her inheritance. She dressed as a harlot and received the Kingdom seed that is listed in the lineage of Jesus in Mathew 1:2.

Boaz was the kinsman redeemer. He was the son of Rahab the harlot, and redeemed an inheritance for Ruth and Naomi.

There is a release of the presence of the Father coming on the earth; it is going to feed the prodigals a meal that will drive them back to the Father. Sons will be granted the robe, ring, and SANDALS, but it's the party at the burning bush that recovers the lost identity. We can't miss the burning bush experiences that will give us an opportunity to remove our sandals, and then have God remove His, and hear Him say, "Walk this way in My shoes, and redeem the harlots, the orphans, the rejected and those still entangled with the bastard curse!" The 11th hour workers are coming, searching for their inheritance. God is going to give Himself to them and they will become sons of God. God started with a family and He will redeem us as a family because that's what Fathers do.

"I hope my journey will help you begin to find your true inheritance."

Blessings,
Charles L. Coker Jr.

Charlie & Susie have traveled for years as itinerant preachers. They are especially called to restore broken marriages, render deliverance from racism, raise levels of faith, impart the maturity of walking in the Father's blessings, and bring freedom from the orphan spirit. They have personally walked through those dry valleys in their own lives and can impart that wisdom and God's word in all of these areas of your life, bringing you to freedom in the Lord.

If you are interested in having them come to your area, contact them through Charlie's website, **www.charliecoker.com.** You can follow his itinerary and his newsletter, and also purchase more books, and other products.

Charlie & Susie are the Senior Pastors at One Kingdom Fellowship, in Deltona, Florida. Check out **www.getgod.org**.

Charlie Coker Ministries
1265 Bramley Lane
Deland, Fl.32720
386-574-8671

www.getgod.org

www. CharlieCoker.com